Synthesis Lectures on Information Concepts, Retrieval, and Services

Series Editor

Gary Marchionini, School of Information and Library Science, The University of North Carolina at Chapel Hill, Chapel Hill, USA

This series publishes short books on topics pertaining to information science and applications of technology to information discovery, production, distribution, and management. Potential topics include: data models, indexing theory and algorithms, classification, information architecture, information economics, privacy and identity, scholarly communication, bibliometrics and webometrics, personal information management, human information behavior, digital libraries, archives and preservation, cultural informatics, information retrieval evaluation, data fusion, relevance feedback, recommendation systems, question answering, natural language processing for retrieval, text summarization, multimedia retrieval, multilingual retrieval, and exploratory search.

Heather O'Brien

User Engagement Research and Practice

 Springer

Heather O'Brien
University of British Columbia
Vancouver, Canada

ISSN 1947-945X   ISSN 1947-9468   (electronic)
Synthesis Lectures on Information Concepts, Retrieval, and Services
ISBN 978-3-031-80915-6   ISBN 978-3-031-80916-3   (eBook)
https://doi.org/10.1007/978-3-031-80916-3

This Springer imprint is published by the registered company Springer Nature Switzerland AG
The registered company address is: Gewerbestrasse 11, 6330 Cham, Switzerland

If disposing of this product, please recycle the paper.

For Elaine, who started the user engagement journey with me. Happy retirement.

And for Silas and Paul, who keep me going and remind me what matters most.

Preface

I have been studying user engagement for the past 20 years. It has always been a slippery concept. Early in my research, people asked me how I would possibly define and measure user engagement, and how to design engaging systems. During those early years, I sought a "solution" to the engagement challenge. I wanted to craft a single definition and a measurement instrument that could be used in multiple settings to evaluate engaging outcomes. I have had some success with these aims, but my quest for a universal way of thinking about, measuring, and designing for engagement has shifted.

Today, if I am asked how to define, measure and design for user engagement, I will tell you "It depends." It depends on the context in which we are studying engagement (Is it health, gaming, searching?), the people we are designing for (Are they tech savvy? What are they trying to accomplish?), and what interactive possibilities are afforded by the technology (How does it enable content consumption or creation, or connecting and communicating with others?).

Why the change? Over time, I have become more comfortable with uncertainty and hopefully wiser about the limits of binary thinking. I have also gained terrific insights from working with other researchers and practitioners. These collaborations have stretched disciplines, and the projects have had different goals (e.g., build a high-quality app to support quality of life outcomes, increase equitable access to information) and have used different methods, ranging from qualitative interviewing and participatory methods to experimental studies and surveys.

While I, as a scholar, have moved away from a universal way of understanding engagement, it feels as though the rest of the world is running toward it. When we hear "user engagement" in today's dynamic technology landscape, our thoughts go to getting and keeping people's attention and maximizing time on a device or application and the usage metrics that are proxies for that attention. Thus, user engagement has come to be defined as a metric rather than an experience, and, in many digital spaces, it is a profit driver rather than a pathway to meaningful outcomes for technology users.

The goal of this book is to promote a more holistic way of thinking about user engagement. In the following chapters, I provide the reader with multiple definitions, theoretical frameworks, methodological approaches, and examples of research studies that describe user engagement in different settings and with different digital information systems. I also consider some of the broader influences on user engagement of emerging technologies. Realizing this goal has been a tall order.

Like many technology-related topics, user engagement has exploded over the past 20 years. It is studied in engineering, computer science, library and information science, communications, media studies, psychology, education and health. Industry and academic authors write about measuring and designing for engagement, and technologies of interest range in focus (e.g., learning, searching, gaming, entertainment, health) and format (apps, haptics, virtual and augmented reality).

It is no longer possible to comprehensively review the literature on user engagement. In preparation for writing this manuscript, two distinct literature reviews were conducted. Both used academic databases in library and information studies, communications, computer science and other cognate fields, with additional hand searching and forward/backward chaining of key works. First, as part of an independent study course, Kin Man Leung (former UBC MLIS student) conducted a systematic review of methods and measures used in user engagement research. She discovered over 800 papers published between 2010 and 2022! Since the book covers more than methods and measures, I conducted a second literature review that broadened the scope but reduced the date parameters (2016–2023); this retrieved over 500 items. I have continued to keep my eyes open for emerging research as I have been writing these chapters. Despite the large volume of studies retrieved in my searches, there are countless studies that are not included because they are conducted by industry and not published.

Given that an exhaustive synthesis was not possible, I have been strategic about what to include and exclude. Since there are two previous works on user engagement (*Measuring User Engagement* by Lalmas, O'Brien and Yom-Tov, 2014; *Why Engagement Matters* edited by O'Brien and Cairns, 2016), I leaned into more recent works (2016–present) in this publication. However, as a former librarian, I always encourage people to go to the original sources and honor early contributors to a research space. So, I have gone back in time when I felt it was needed, such as explaining the origins of engagement and its theoretical underpinnings. Adding to the issue of volume, information interactions are threaded throughout all digital environments. This raised scope issues for the current work and forced some challenging decisions about what domains to include. In the end, the reader will have a healthy bibliography on user engagement with digital information systems and can branch off into specific subject areas like health and education depending on their needs.

User engagement research is rapidly changing because our world and our technologies are rapidly changing. Maybe we will need a new synthesis lecture in a year, maybe five? For now, this is a snapshot of where we are and, upon solid reflection, where we might strive to go.

Vancouver, Canada   Heather O'Brien
July 2024

Acknowledgements

This book project received funding support from a SSHRC Explore Grant: Arts Research from the University of British Columbia (Award Number: AWD-024749 SSHRC 2023).

I am grateful to the many colleagues and students I have collaborated with over 20 years of researching user engagement. You have helped me think more deeply about my work, and it has been such a privilege to publish with many of you.

This book would not have reached the finish line without the extraordinary talents of Nilou Davoudi, who provided research assistance and editing. Nilou, you are an amazing and generous person and scholar, and it is such an honor to be part of your academic journey.

Contents

This morning, I am drinking coffee as I move from one game to another on the *New York Times* app. I get stuck on Connections, the word association game. Across the kitchen table from me, my tween is on YouTube. We are waking up slowly. Alone. Together[1].

It is hard not to be distracted by the YouTube video my son is watching. "Survive 100 days trapped, win $500,00" is on Day 60 (MrBeast, 2023). Contestants Suzie and Bailey have just turned down the mystery box MrBeast was offering (Miller & Hogg, 2023). The audience knows there's a Tesla on offer and the contestants would have also gotten back the $50,000 "cost" of saying yes to the offer. Suzie is especially devastated. Bailey says he's happy with his Prius. Only 40 more days to go in their little surveillance cubicle in the middle of nowhere. I bet they say "yes" to the next offer. I hold back my "mom-entary" in case he takes his Cheerios to the living room. Better to know what he's watching.

I check my email. Six new messages in the last 10 minutes. Delete one, quick response to two. Three will take more time since I can't type well on my phone. I know I will look at it when I get to work, and it will take longer than I think to deal with. I will never get this book written.

I am nursing my coffee. I scan my Google news feed. More stories about cell phone bans in local schools and whether we need warnings on social media. I click on an article in *The Conversation Canada*. Three academic researchers are debating the pros and cons. I pause, "[social media] platforms create and design features to maximize usage, profiting from user engagement" (Deneault et al., 2024). User engagement. It's become a buzz word for eyeballs glued to screens.

---

[1] Sherry Turkle (2010). Alone together. NY: Basic Books.

© The Author(s), under exclusive license to Springer Nature Switzerland AG 2025   1
H. O'Brien, *User Engagement Research and Practice*, Synthesis Lectures on Information Concepts, Retrieval, and Services, https://doi.org/10.1007/978-3-031-80916-3_1

Day 70. Suzie and Bailey are eating dinner and debating the latest offer. We move to MrBeast plugging Shop App. We ping pong back and forth between the contestants and Shop App. It is not clear where the ad begins and ends.

So much for leaving for work by 8.

1.1   How Did We Get Here?

In 2004, I started my doctoral program at Dalhousie University to study health information-seeking behavior. I pivoted in the first few months after my curiosity was piqued in a research talk where the speaker kept using the term "user engagement." I turned to my supervisor, Dr. Elaine Toms. "What does he mean by user engagement?" I asked. "You're a librarian," she replied, "Look it up!"

So, like any good librarian, I dove into the literature from education, human-computer interaction, psychology, management and information science looking for the answer to the question, "What is user engagement?" (O'Brien & Toms, 2008).

I found that user engagement had been in use for some time. In 1986, Don Norman talked about *direct engagement*, whereby users translate their psychological intentions into physical actions that can be carried out with technology (Norman, 1986). Brenda Laurel's book, *Computers as Theatre*, argued that a digital interface is more than a place where "a person and a computer represent themselves to one another; rather it is a shared context for action in which both are *agents*" [emphasis mine] (p. 4). Laurel called user engagement "a state of mind" and likened the user experience to an unfolding drama full of emotion, imagination, "carefully crafted uncertainty," and a satisfying outcome (p. 67). Kearsley and Schneiderman (1998) talked about engaged learners being intrinsically motivated and self-directed in constructing knowledge. Jacques, Carey and Preece (1995) and Webster and Ho (1997) both studied how students interacted with multimedia and tested out what "ingredients" might make these interactions engaging, e.g., being in control of the interaction, well timed feedback from the technology, aesthetically pleasing and interactive features.

User engagement research is nestled in human-computer interaction, a field charted through a succession of "waves." Bødker (2015) identified the first wave as "model-driven and focused on the human being as a subject to be studied through rigid guidelines, formal methods, and systematic testing," followed by a movement to workplace settings and collaboration in the second wave that prioritized efficiency and effectiveness (p. 24).[2] The period of the first and second waves (1985–2005) was "the personal computing era...marked by the spread of Internet and intranet use, graphical user interfaces, and the World Wide Web" (Grudin, 2005, p. 53). The transition to third wave HCI acknowledged

---

[2] While Bødker indicates the first wave was rooted in human factors and cognition, Harrison et al., (2007, p. 12) discuss the waves as "paradigms," mapping the first wave to human factors, the second wave to cognitivism/information processing, and the third wave as phenomenologically situated.

the increased use of technologies in everyday life settings, the role of content, emotion and culture in technology use and evaluation, and multimethod approaches (Bødker, 2006; Harrison et al., 2007). During the early to mid-2000s, new outcome measures for human-computer interaction concepts emerged, including aesthetics (Lavie & Tractinsky, 2004), immersion (Brown & Cairns, 2004), transcendence (Laarni et al., 2004), cognitive absorption (Agarwal & Karahanna, 2000), and fun (Blythe et al., 2003). User experience became the new research agenda (Hassenzahl & Tractinsky, 2006; McCarthy & Wright, 2007) and a backdrop for my own dissertation work on user engagement (O'Brien, 2008).

Fast forward 20 years to 2024. Almost 70% of the global population owns a smartphone, 5.44 billion people (67.1%) use the Internet and 5.07 billion (62.6%) use at least one social media platform (Statista, 2024). Google has long dominated the online search market (Statista, 2024a), but search is being transformed in unexpected ways due to advances in artificial intelligence (Shah & Bender, 2022). OpenAI launched its chatbot and virtual assistant, ChatGPT, in November 2022 (*Introducing* ChatGPT, 2024). ChatGPT (and similar products) are being used like search engines with definite downsides. ChatGPT has been criticized for producing "fresh falsehoods" and "inaccurate information" (Knight, 2023), based on the "garbage in, garbage out" model of the Internet; the uptick of "phantom references" reinforces this critique (Karpf, 2023). Beyond ChatGPT, AI-enabled search engines are hitting the market, including Perplexity and SearchGPT, with the goal of not only producing search results, but supporting users in their information sense making (Robison, 2024). In other words, these products will allow us to further outsource thinking about and evaluating information. Social media platforms continue to be popular information sources. TikTok, the fastest growing social media platform (Ceci, 2024), uses its personalized videos and storytelling format to negate the need for traditional search engines (Adobe Express, 2024).

So, if in the past we were in an era of personal computing or user experience, we must certainly now be riding a new wave of algorithmic engagement. Content and interface interactions are superseded by trying to shape the algorithms that feed us news, entertainment and information (Abidin, 2020), "content without context" (Bhandari & Bimo, 2022, p. 8), engagement without agency (O'Brien et al., 2022).

1.2 Defining User Engagement

User engagement is a ubiquitous term that means different things to different people. It has been used synonymously with terms like usability, adherence, participation, interactivity, and attention (Johnston, 2018; O'Brien, 2008; Perugia et al., 2022), and sometimes narrowly and inconsistently defined (Cunningham et al., 2024; O'Brien, 2016; Perski et al., 2017). Definitions can offer language to communicate about a construct, especially one like user engagement that stretches across disciplines and digital domains. Definitions can also provide structure and scope for evaluating or designing for user engagement.

For example, if we define engagement as user behavior, then measures like duration and frequency of use make perfect sense; however, if we think of engagement as having emotional or cognitive elements, then these measures are severely limited. It is appealing to strive for a universal definition, and, admittedly, I once thought this was possible. Over time, however, I have recognized that engagement is not "plug-and-play." It is informed by the "larger set of values, contexts, and disciplinary perspectives that inform human relationships with technology" (O'Brien, 2016, p. 1).

A longstanding idea is that engagement has cognitive, affective and behavioral elements (Constantiou et al., 2022; Dvir, 2020; Jacques, 1996; Lalmas et al., 2014; Laurel, 1993; O'Brien, 2016; O'Brien & Toms, 2008; Oh & Sundar, 2015; Webster & Ho, 1997); this is derived from research in school settings focused on the holistic interaction of students' attitudes, behaviors and emotions that contribute to learning and social outcomes (Fredricks et al., 2004). Cognitive aspects of engagement include attention, awareness, and mental effort; emotional engagement encompasses subjective aspects of identity, belonging, values, attitudes or positive and negative emotions, e.g., interest, boredom; and behavioral engagement is an objective manifestation of (inter)action and participation (Doherty & Doherty, 2019; O'Brien & Toms, 2008; Oh et al., 2018).

Despite the seeming agreement that user engagement is affective, cognitive, and behavioral in nature, it is increasingly defined and operationalized as a behavioral "signal…an action taken by a user on an item, e.g. click, like, comment, retweet, upvote, downvote dwell time, watch time" (Cunningham et al., 2024, p. 2). The emphasis on usage not only ignores important individual and contextual parts of the user experience, but it also creates an "engagement-for-engagement's-sake" atmosphere that quantifies rather than qualifies engagement (Halverson & Graham, 2019; Kuntsman & Miyake, 2022; O'Brien et al., 2022). An example of this can be found in the vast literature on mis/disinformation showing that people interact with and share information they do not believe to be true (Edelson et al., 2021), especially when emotional valence is high (Spiro & Starbird, 2023). Weber et al. (2023) use "reflective engagement" as a counter point to such actions and reactions, considering the ways in which people might be encouraged to reflect on their beliefs and assumptions and consider opposing viewpoints.

Definitions of user engagement

Many definitions of user engagement have been proposed. Doherty and Doherty's (2019) review of 350+ papers in the ACM Digital Library revealed that papers that defined user engagement (only 35%) included both general and context specific definitions. The following is a selection of definitions that have appeared over time (in chronological order):

- "The state of mind that we must attain in order to enjoy a representation of an action" so that we may experience computer worlds "directly, without mediation or distraction" (Laurel, 1993, p. 112–113, 116).

- "A user's response to an interaction that gains, maintains, and encourages their attention, particularly when they are intrinsically motivated" (Jacques et al., 1995, p. 103).
- "A quality of user experiences with technology that is characterized by challenge, aesthetic and sensory appeal, feedback, novelty, interactivity, perceived control and time, awareness, motivation, interest, and affect" (O'Brien & Toms, 2008, p. 949).
- "The emotional, cognitive, and behavioral experience of a user with a technological resource that exists, at any point in time and over time" (Lalmas et al., 2014, p. 3).
- "A quality of UX that is characterized by the depth of the actor's investment in the interaction; this investment may be defined temporally, emotionally, and/or cognitively" (O'Brien, 2016, p. 22).
- "A dynamic multidimensional relational concept featuring psychological and behavioral attributes of connection, interaction, participation, and involvement, designed to achieve or elicit an outcome at individual, organization, or social levels" (Johnston, 2018, p. 19).
- "The degree of participation in a playful activity that can take different hedonic tones (negative to positive valence) and achieve different levels of energy mobilization (low to high arousal)" (Perugia et al., 2022, p. 940).

In these definitions, engagement is depicted as a trait, state and process (Doherty & Doherty, 2019). Trait-based approaches look at a person's propensity to be engaged based on some individual characteristics, such as personality or cognitive absorption. Engagement as a state is based on the temporal, dynamic aspects of experience (Johnston, 2018). Finally, engagement as a process enables researchers to reflect on how users engage across time and modes of interaction (O'Brien & Toms, 2008).

While these definitions differ, we can see some commonalities, namely the mention of cognitive, affective and behavioral components, the emphasis on attributes that might be part of an engaging experience (e.g., attention, interest, participation), and the dynamism of engagement, both in the moment and over time. My own definitions of engagement have evolved. Most recently, my colleagues and I reconsidered the notion of "disengagement" as something more than the end of engagement. We envisioned engagement and disengagement in a more symbiotic relationship where user agency and goals determine the value of the end-user experience (O'Brien et al., 2022).

How we define engagement points at who and what matters in human-computer interactions. Health researchers view "effective engagement" as the link between in-app and out-of-app experiences, where using a digital application helps bring about a desired health change or outcome; multiple and diverse indicators are needed to understand the extent to which the digital tool makes a difference (Cole-Lewis et al., 2019; Michie et al., 2017, p. 8).

Yet, increasingly, definitions of engagement have become rather flat and one dimensional, focusing on "clicks and downloads" (O'Brien et al., 2020a, 2020b) rather than holistic experiences—less process and more product driven. When engagement is mediating the relationships between people, technology, and desired outcomes (e.g., learning, health and well-being), we are prioritizing the user experience; when engagement is the end goal, it is the metrics that matter, and context becomes a way to optimize attention and profit (Srnicek, 2017). Both scenarios are value laden and actively playing out right now.

1.3   Scoping User Engagement Research

One of the biggest questions I contended with in writing this book was domain. I am an information scientist, but have always drawn upon many disciplines to situate my work. Engagement stretches across many disciplines and technologies, but my main interest is in the diverse technologies people use to access and share information. News comes from traditional news outlets, e.g., *The New York Times*, but also through social media like Facebook; people query Siri and Alexa (and increasingly, ChatGPT and Perplexity.ai) rather than opening a web browser. Information systems cover a broad swath of technologies, so I considered information retrieval as a core function.

Information retrieval (IR) systems facilitate the organization, storage and searching of document collections (text, multimedia, images). Collectively, IR systems support indexing, which involves inputting documents and information about the documents, i.e., metadata like title, keywords, etc., to facilitate access. The second important process is retrieval. To provide a user with information that meets their needs, user queries must be transformed in a way that can be compared with indexed information (Larson, 2012). (For more in-depth information about information retrieval systems including how they work and their role in information seeking, please see White's (2016) comprehensive text, *Interactions with Search Systems* or *Understanding Information Retrieval Systems: Management, Types, and Standards* edited by Bates (2012)).

For this book's purposes, research was included about social media; general web search engines, digital cultural heritage collections; online news websites; interactive media, and intelligent agents[3].

Types of Information Systems

- *Social media* includes social networking sites (e.g., Facebook), microblogging sites (Twitter, now X), and content communities (e.g., YouTube) and are a source for news,

---

[3] People also access information through other systems, such as digital health interventions (DHI). DHIs encompass websites, mobile devices, telemedicine, wearables) and are built for different audiences (patients, caregivers, clinicians, health administrators) (World Health Organization, 2019) to achieve specific, measurable health objectives (World Health Organization, 2018). While I include some research and examples from the health field, this area was not incorporated in-depth due to scoping issues.

entertainment and information sharing worldwide. Each platform attracts a unique user demographic (Gottfried, 2024). Research on social media engagement tends to focus on specific communities (e.g., citizens of a certain country who engage with specific social media platforms (e.g., TikTok, WhatsApp), along with what users are engaging with and how the platforms' design affordances sustain engagement. Social media platforms feature multimedia, e.g., memes, videos, images, and music, which create different possibilities for engagement.

- *Web search engines* are software that crawls and gathers hyperlinks to Internet webpages in response to users' queries. Search engines have four components: (1) mechanisms to compile webpages for inclusion in their databases; (2) indexing programs to extract metadata from the webpages; (3) searching and ranking algorithms that determine what results are presented to users in response to queries; and (4) user interfaces. The interface allows users to query the system, typically using natural language keywords or phrases, and view a list of retrieved web pages (i.e., the search engine results page (SERP)) (Hock, 2012). The SERP may contain additional information about the retrieved results, such as text or visual summaries or snippets of the content, and provide suggestions for query modification or narrowing search results (e.g., date parameters). Common search engines include Google, Bing, Baidu and GoDuckGo.

- *Digital libraries* hosted by libraries, archives and museums support digital preservation and access to special content collections, which may contain items of cultural, historical, or scientific significance to a community, institution or nation (Borgman, 1999). Engagement with digital libraries may present unique challenges for user engagement compared to web search engines because they must balance preservation and discovery goals (Agosti et al., 2018). Different levels of expertise, types of information objects (e.g., language, multimedia format) and specialized document genres (e.g., almanacs, maps) require considerations for document description and information retrieval and use in general (Koolen et al., 2009) and engagement outcomes more specifically.

- The digital environment has significantly shifted how people consume *online news.* About one-third of the Americans continue to get their news from television, but digital devices are overwhelmingly preferred over radio and print news (Pew Research Center, 2023). For those who access news via smartphones, tablets and laptop computers, news sources are diverse. In 2023, US survey respondents said they sometimes or often used news websites or apps (67%), but also social media (50%), search engines (71%), or podcasts (30%) to access news. While news websites and apps may provide more current and in-depth information compared to social media platforms, the speed and convenience of getting news via social media makes it attractive and engaging, despite concerns over accuracy and bias (Wang & Forman-Katz, 2024).

- *Interactive media* are "any computer-delivered electronic system that allows the user to control, combine, and manipulate different types of media, such as text, sound, video, computer graphics, and animation" (Britannica, 2024). This includes interactive film and television, infographics and data visualizations, digital signage, video, toolkits and widgets. Collectively, the use of storytelling and gamification to stimulate user interest is a common theme across these works, as is the connection between information presentation, comprehension and engagement.

- An *intelligent agent* is a technology that "perceives its environment, takes actions autonomously in order to achieve goals, and may improve its performance with learning or acquiring knowledge" ("Intelligent Agent," 2024). This may include conversational agents (chatbots) and digital assistants that are voice or text activated, e.g., Apple's Siri, OpenAI's ChatGPT.

Many of these technologies are what White (2016) refers to as "next-generation search interaction" tools and their rapid evolution is changing the ways in which we locate, process, make sense of and engage with information:

> Advances in data availability coupled with new interaction paradigms (touch, gaze, large displays, gesture, spoken dialogue) and mobile computing capabilities (more powerful tablets, smartphones, and tablets...) have created a broad range of new opportunities for information access and use. People can now interact with search systems in more lightweight and natural ways using modalities such as touch (swipes and pinches on phones and tablets), gesture (on devices such as the Kinect or the Leap), augmented reality, and more accurate speech recognition. (White, 2016, p. xv)

Multi-modality and ubiquity are characteristics of contemporary information interaction and retrieval practices and have implications for engagement that we will explore in the forthcoming chapters.

1.4   Organization of the Book

This book is comprised of six distinct chapters:

Chapter 1, **Introduction**, introduces the book and user engagement, including various definitions of user engagement, and establishes the scope of the research and technologies included.

Chapter 2, **Conceptual Approaches to User Engagement** draws on select theories and models. This chapter is placed early in the book to encourage reflection in later chapters about the research and examples featured.

Chapter 3, **User Engagement with Digital Information Systems** examines qualities of people, information and technologies that contribute to user engagement in information interaction research.

Chapter 4, **Influences on User Engagement**, looks at the broader context in which engagement with digital information systems is unfolding. Specifically, I consider strategies used by persuasive technologies and gamification and their relationship to engagement. I also contemplate how these influences are changing how we engage with technologies using TikTok to illustrate active and passive engagement.

Chapter 5, **Approaches to Measuring User Engagement** profiles the self-report, behavioral, and physiological methods and measures used to investigate user engagement.

Chapter 6, The **Conclusion** considers some grand challenges for user engagement research based on the current state of user engagement research.

References

Abidin, C. (2020). Mapping internet celebrity on TikTok: Exploring attention economies and visibility labours. *Cultural Science Journal, 12*(1), 77–103. https://doi.org/10.5334/csci.140

Agarwal, R., & Karahanna, E. (2000). Time flies when you're having fun: Cognitive absorption and beliefs about information technology usage. *MIS Quarterly, 24*(4), 665–694. https://doi.org/10.2307/3250951

Agosti, M., Orio, N., & Ponchia, C. (2018). Promoting user engagement with digital cultural heritage collections. *International Journal on Digital Libraries, 19*(4), 353–366. https://doi.org/10.1007/s00799-018-0245-y

Adobe Express. (2024). *Using TikTok as a search engine | Adobe express.* https://www.adobe.com/express/learn/blog/using-tiktok-as-a-search-engine

Bates, M. J. (Ed.). (2012). *Understanding information retrieval systems: management, types, and standards* (1st ed.). CRC Press.

Bhandari, A., & Bimo, S. (2022). Why's everyone on TikTok Now? The algorithmized self and the future of self-making on social media. *Social Media and Society, 8*(1), 205630512210862–205630512210862. https://doi.org/10.1177/20563051221086241

Blythe, M. A., Monk, A. F., Overbeeke, K., & Wright, P. C. (Eds.). (2003). *Funology: From usability to enjoyment* (Vol. 3). Kluwer Academic Publisher.

Bødker, S. (2015). Third-wave HCI, 10 years later—Participation and sharing. *Interactions, 22*(5), 24–31. https://doi.org/10.1145/2804405

Bødker, S. (2006). When second wave HCI meets third wave challenges. *Proceedings of the 4th Nordic Conference on Human-Computer Interaction: Changing Roles* (pp. 1–8). https://doi.org/10.1145/1182475.1182476

Borgman, C. L. (1999). What are digital libraries? Competing visions. *Information Processing and Management, 35*(3), 227–243. https://doi.org/10.1016/S0306-4573(98)00059-4

Britannica. (2024, May 13). *Interactive media.* Encyclopedia Britannica. https://www.britannica.com/technology/interactive-media

Brown, E., & Cairns, P. (2004). A grounded investigation of game immersion. *CHI '04 Extended Abstracts on Human Factors in Computing Systems* (pp. 1297–1300). https://doi.org/10.1145/985921.986048

Ceci, L. (2024, April). *Topic: TikTok.* Statista. https://www.statista.com/topics/6077/tiktok/

Introducing ChatGPT. (2024). https://openai.com/index/chatgpt/

Cole-Lewis, H., Ezeanochie, N., & Turgiss, J. (2019). Understanding health behavior technology engagement: Pathway to measuring digital behavior change interventions. *JMIR Formative Research, 3*(4), e14052. https://doi.org/10.2196/14052

Constantiou, I., Mukkamala, A., Sjöklint, M., & Trier, M. (2022). Engaging with self-tracking applications: How do users respond to their performance data? *European Journal of Information Systems, 0*(0), 1–21. https://doi.org/10.1080/0960085X.2022.2081096

Cunningham, T., Pandey, S., Sigerson, L., Stray, J., Allen, J., Barrilleaux, B., Iyer, R., Milli, S., Kothari, M., & Rezaei, B. (2024). *What we know about using non-engagement signals in content ranking* (arXiv:2402.06831). arXiv. https://doi.org/10.48550/arXiv.2402.06831

Deneault, A.-A., Madigan, S., & Vaillancourt, T. (2024, June 20). *Social media warning labels and school cell phone bans: Do they unlock better youth mental health?* The Conversation. http://theconversation.com/social-media-warning-labels-and-school-cell-phone-bans-do-they-unlock-better-youth-mental-health-232890

Doherty, K., & Doherty, G. (2019). Engagement in HCI: Conception, theory and measurement. *ACM Computing Surveys, 51*(5), 1–39. https://doi.org/10.1145/3234149

Dvir, N. (2020). Process of information engagement: Integrating information behavior and user engagement. *Proceedings of the Association for Information Science and Technology, 57*(1), e407. https://doi.org/10.1002/pra2.407

Edelson, L., Nguyen, M.-K., Goldstein, I., Goga, O., McCoy, D., & Lauinger, T. (2021). Understanding engagement with U.S. (mis)information news sources on Facebook. *Proceedings of the 21st ACM Internet Measurement Conference* (pp. 444–463). https://doi.org/10.1145/3487552.3487859

Fredricks, J. A., Blumenfeld, P. C., & Paris, A. H. (2004). School engagement: Potential of the concept, state of the evidence. *Review of Educational Research, 74*(1), 59–109.

Gottfried, J. (2024, January 31). Americans' social media use. *Pew Research Center.* https://www.pewresearch.org/internet/2024/01/31/americans-social-media-use/

Grudin, J. (2005). Three faces of human-computer interaction. *IEEE Annals of the History of Computing, 27*(4), 46–62. https://doi.org/10.1109/MAHC.2005.67

Halverson, L. R., & Graham, C. R. (2019). Learner engagement in blended learning environments: A conceptual framework. *Online Learning, 23*(2). https://doi.org/10.24059/olj.v23i2.1481

Harrison, S., Tatar, D., & Sengers, P. (2007). The three paradigms of HCI. *CHI 2007.* Alt. Chi. session at SIGCHI conference on human factors in computing systems, San Jose.

Hassenzahl, M., & Tractinsky, N. (2006). User experience—A research agenda. *Behaviour and Information Technology, 25*(2), 91–97. https://doi.org/10.1080/01449290500330331

Hock, R. (2012). Search engines. In M. J. Bates (Ed.), *Understanding information retrieval systems: Management, types, and standards* (1st ed). CRC Press, Taylor and Francis Group.

Jacques, R., Preece, J., & Carey, T. (1995). Engagement as a design concept for multimedia. *Canadian Journal of Learning and Technology.* https://doi.org/10.21432/T2VG77

Jacques, R. D. (1996). *The nature of engagement and its role in hypermedia evaluation and design* [Doctoral Dissertation]. South Bank University.

Johnston, K. A. (2018). Toward a theory of social engagement. In K. A. Johnston & M. Taylor (Eds.), *The handbook of communication engagement* (pp.17-32). Wiley & Sons, Inc. https://doi.org/10.1002/9781119167600.ch2

Karpf, D. (2023, March 20). On generative AI, phantom citations, and social calluses [Substack newsletter]. *The Future, Now and Then.* https://davekarpf.substack.com/p/on-generative-ai-phantom-citations

Kearsley, G., & Shneiderman, B. (1998). Engagement theory: A framework for technology-based teaching and learning. *Educational Technology, 38,* 20–23.

Knight, W. (2023). The race to build a ChatGPT-powered search engine. *Wired.* https://www.wired.com/story/the-race-to-build-a-chatgpt-powered-search-engine/

Koolen, M., Kamps, J., & de Keijzer, V. (2009). Information retrieval in cultural heritage. *Interdisciplinary Science Reviews, 34*(2–3), 268–284. https://doi.org/10.1179/174327909X441153

Kuntsman, A., & Miyake, E. (2022). *Paradoxes of digital disengagement: In search of the opt-out button.* University of Westminster Press. https://doi.org/10.16997/book61

Laarni, J., Ravaja, N., Kallinen, K., & Saari, T. (2004). Transcendent experience in the use of computer-based media. In *NordiCHI Third Nordic Conference on Human-Computer Interaction, Tampere, Finland, October 23-27, 2004* (pp. 409–412). ACM. https://research.aalto.fi/en/public ations/transcendent-experience-in-the-use-of-computer-based-media

Lalmas, M., O'Brien, H., & Yom-Tov, E. (2014). Measuring user engagement. In *Synthesis lectures on information concepts, retrieval, and services* (Vol. 6). https://doi.org/10.2200/S00605ED1V01 Y201410ICR038

Larson, R. (2012). Information retrieval systems. In M. J. Bates (Ed.), *Understanding information retrieval systems: Management, types, and standards.* (1st ed). CRC Press, Taylor and Francis Group.

Laurel, B. (1993). *Computers as theatre.* Addison-Wesley.

Lavie, T., & Tractinsky, N. (2004). Assessing dimensions of perceived visual aesthetics of web sites. *International Journal of Human-Computer Studies, 60*(3), 269–298. https://doi.org/10.1016/j. ijhcs.2003.09.002

McCarthy, J., & Wright, P. (2007). *Technology as experience.* MIT Press. https://mitpress.mit.edu/ 9780262633550/technology-as-experience/

Michie, S., Yardley, L., West, R., Patrick, K., & Greaves, F. (2017). Developing and evaluating digital interventions to promote behavior change in health and health care: Recommendations resulting from an international workshop. *Journal of Medical Internet Research, 19*(6), e232. https://doi. org/10.2196/jmir.7126

Miller, V., & Hogg, E. (2023). 'If you press this, I'll pay': MrBeast, YouTube, and the mobilisation of the audience commodity in the name of charity. *Convergence, 29*(4), 997–1014. https://doi. org/10.1177/13548565231161810

MrBeast (Director). (2023, December 17). *Survive 100 Days Trapped, Win $500,000.* https://www. youtube.com/watch?v=9RhWXPcKBI8

Norman, D. A. (1986). Cognitive engineering. In D. A. Norman & S. W. Draper (Eds.), *User centred system design* (pp. 31–61). Lawrence Erlbaum Associates. https://ics.uci.edu/~redmiles/inf233-FQ07/oldpapers/Norman1986ch3.pdf

O'Brien, H. L. (2016). Translating theory into methodological practice. In H. O'Brien & P. Cairns (Eds.), *Why engagement matters: Cross-disciplinary perspectives of user engagement in digital media* (pp. 27–52). Springer Cham.

O'Brien, H. L., & Toms, E. G. (2008). What is user engagement? A conceptual framework for defining user engagement with technology. *Journal of the American Society for Information Science and Technology, 59*(6), 938–955. https://doi.org/10.1002/asi.20801

O'Brien, H. L., Arguello, J., & Capra, R. (2020a). An empirical study of interest, task complexity, and search behaviour on user engagement. *Information Processing and Management, 57*(3), 102226.

O'Brien, H. L., Roll, I., Kampen, A., & Davoudi, N. (2022). Rethinking (Dis)engagement in human-computer interaction. *Computers in Human Behavior, 128*, 107109. https://doi.org/10.1016/j.chb. 2021.107109

O'Brien, H. L, Morton, E., Kampen, A., Barnes, S. J., & Michalak, E. E. (2020). Beyond clicks and downloads: A call for a more comprehensive approach to measuring mobile-health app engagement. *BJPsych Open, 6*(5), e86. https://doi.org/10.1192/bjo.2020.72

O'Brien, H. L. (2008). *Defining and measuring engagement in user experiences with technology* [Doctoral Dissertation]. Dalhousie University.

Oh, J., & Sundar, S. S. (2015). How does interactivity persuade? An experimental test of interactivity on cognitive absorption, elaboration, and attitudes. *Journal of Communication, 65*(2), 213–236. https://doi.org/10.1111/jcom.12147

Oh, J., Bellur, S., & Sundar, S. S. (2018). Clicking, assessing, immersing, and sharing: An empirical model of user engagement with interactive media. *Communication Research, 45*(5), 737–763. https://doi.org/10.1177/0093650215600493

Perski, O., Blandford, A., West, R., & Michie, S. (2017). Conceptualising engagement with digital behaviour change interventions: A systematic review using principles from critical interpretive synthesis. *Translational Behavioral Medicine, 7*(2), 254–267. https://doi.org/10.1007/s13142-016-0453-1

Perugia, G., Díaz-Boladeras, M., Català-Mallofré, A., Barakova, E. I., & Rauterberg, M. (2022). ENGAGE-DEM: A model of engagement of people with dementia. *IEEE Transactions on Affective Computing, 13*(2), 926–943. https://doi.org/10.1109/TAFFC.2020.2980275

Pew Research Center. (2023, November). *News Platform Fact Sheet.* https://www.pewresearch.org/journalism/fact-sheet/news-platform-fact-sheet/

Robison, K. (2024). OpenAI announces SearchGPT, its AI-powered search engine. *The Verge, July 25, 2024,* https://www.theverge.com/2024/7/25/24205701/openai-searchgpt-ai-search-engine-google-perplexity-riva

Shah, C., & Bender, E. M. (2022). Situating search. *ACM SIGIR Conference on Human Information Interaction and Retrieval* (pp. 221–232). https://doi.org/10.1145/3498366.3505816

Spiro, E., & Starbird, K. (2023, May 11). Rumors Have Rules. *Issues in Science and Technology.* https://issues.org/rumors-research-misinformation-spiro-starbird/

Srnicek, N. (2017). The challenges of platform capitalism: Understanding the logic of a new business model. *Juncture, 23*(4), 254–257.

Statista. (2024, February). *Global search engine desktop market share 2024.* Statista. https://www.statista.com/statistics/216573/worldwide-market-share-of-search-engines/

Statista. (2024a, June 12). *Topic: Smartphones.* Statista. https://www.statista.com/topics/840/smartphones/

Turkle, S. (2010). *Alone together.* Basic Books.

Wang, L., & Forman-Katz, N. (2024, February 7). Many Americans find value in getting news on social media, but concerns about inaccuracy have risen. *Pew Research Center.* https://www.pewresearch.org/short-reads/2024/02/07/many-americans-find-value-in-getting-news-on-social-media-but-concerns-about-inaccuracy-have-risen/

Weber, K., Aicher, A., Minker, W., Ultes, S., & André, E. (2023). Fostering user engagement in the critical reflection of arguments. arXiv preprint arXiv:2308.09061.

Webster, J., & Ho, H. (1997). Audience engagement in multimedia presentations. *ACM SIGMIS Database: the DATABASE for Advances in Information Systems, 28*(2), 63–77. https://doi.org/10.1145/264701.264706

White, R. W. (2016). Interactions with search systems. *Cambridge University Press.* https://doi.org/10.1017/CBO9781139525305

World Health Organization. (2018). *Classification of digital health interventions v1.0: A shared language to describe the uses of digital technology for health* (WHO/RHR/18.06). Article WHO/RHR/18.06. https://iris.who.int/handle/10665/260480

World Health Organization. (2019). *WHO guideline Recommendations on Digital Interventions for Health System Strengthening.* World Health Organization. http://www.ncbi.nlm.nih.gov/books/NBK541902/

"There is nothing so practical as a good theory"

– Kurt Lewin (1943)

In the introduction to a special issue of the *Educational Psychologist* on "Engagement in the Context of Science Learning," Azevedo (2015) observed that "none of [the articles in the special issue] adhere to a particular theory of engagement because there is none" (p. 88). This statement raises a lot of questions. *What do we mean by "theory"? Do we even need theory to study user engagement? Does this mean that user engagement research is devoid of theory, or is there no theory that can adequately explain it?*

The term theory is challenging because it can mean "everything from minor working hypotheses, through comprehensive but vague and unordered speculations, to axiomatic systems of thought" (Merton, 1968, p. 39). Indeed, some classifications of "theoretical frameworks" include theories, models and even measurement instruments (Doherty & Doherty, 2019).[1]

Theory is often grounded in a particular paradigm. A paradigm is "the entire constellation of beliefs, values, techniques, and so on shared by members of a given [scientific] community" (Kuhn, 1970, as cited in Pickard, 2013, p. 6). Paradigms typically ask

---

[1] Doherty and Doherty (2019) observed 372 mentions of theoretical frameworks in their systematic review of 351 computer science journal and conference papers. These included a range of diverse items, include Self-Determination Theory, Immersive Tendencies Questionnaire, and various models of engagement.

H. O'Brien, *User Engagement Research and Practice*, Synthesis Lectures on Information Concepts, Retrieval, and Services, https://doi.org/10.1007/978-3-031-80916-3_2

researchers to answer the following questions: "What is the nature of reality?" (ontology); "What is the relationship between the knower and the known?" (epistemology); and "How do we come to know?" (methodology) (Lincoln & Guba, 1985). How we answer these questions defines our worldview or our "basic set of beliefs that guide action" (Creswell, 2014, p. 6). Examples of paradigms include (post-) positivism, constructivism, and pragmatism (Creswell, 2014), and set researchers on different paths when it comes to articulating research questions, gathering and making sense of data, engaging with research participants, and situating their work in broader societal forces. Theory takes on different roles depending on the researchers' paradigm or world view. It can be "a priori," where hypotheses are generated based on existing research; it can emerge inductively from the data; and it can be used to critique observations based on social inequities or power structures (Cooksey & McDonald, 2019).

Research can also take place without theory, i.e., "straightforward description" (Cooksey & McDonald, 2019, p. 253), but this can be limiting. In the case of user engagement,

> Theory helps us make sense of users' experiences: it informs how we design studies and interfaces; it allows us to derive and model user, system, and contextual factors that predict [user engagement] UE; and it places expected and unexpected outcomes of user studies and design experiments into a broader interpretive framework. (O'Brien, 2016, p. 9)

I would argue that it is the lack of conceptual grounding that has contributed to the shifting of user engagement from a multidimensional construct to a mere metric. A theme in this book is that engagement is increasingly being defined as a measure, e.g., "an action taken by a user on an item" (Cunningham et al., 2024). This is at odds with accepted definitions of engagement that consider it a quality of experience with cognitive, emotional, and behavioral components (see Chap. 1, Definitions). Theoretical framing can help us capture the richness that is lost when we define something according to what we can most easily and "objectively" measure.

Even if we agree that we need theory in user engagement research, no one theory may fully help us understand or explain user engagement because it is a multidisciplinary phenomenon. Its study has been shaped by the paradigms, theories and research traditions of scholars from many fields, including education, marketing, health, psychology, library and information studies, communications, engineering, and computer science.

Another important term to consider when thinking about theory is model. According to Bates (2005), models "can often help in working through one's thinking about a subject of interest" (p. 3) and may be building blocks in theory development. Models can be graphical, formulaic, or text-based representations about how something works or how different concepts and ideas are connected (Fidel, 2012). Models can be purely conceptual, but there are also measurement models that use statistical techniques. Many models of user engagement have been proposed, and this chapter will look at a selection of representative models.

The goal of the chapter is not to insist that the reader use the theories or models depicted here. Nor is it to claim that theories are not without their limitations; for instance, connecting theory to how things unfold in the real world is sometimes difficult. But conceptual frameworks can act as anchors and guides when we design and carry out research studies, they can increase our power to explain and communicate research findings, and they can help us trace changes over time in how engagement with digital technologies is being experienced and designed for.

2.1   Demystifying User Engagement: Theoretical Underpinnings

This chapter highlights a selection of theories, specifically Flow Theory and Uses and Gratifications Theory (U&G), applied to the study of engagement. Flow Theory is rooted in phenomenological psychology and U&G was developed in mass communications. Both theories center affective (e.g., motivation) and cognitive (e.g., attention) elements, rather than focusing solely on technology or media use behaviors. Media use is motivated intrinsically, in the case of Flow Theory, and for various reasons (like information or entertainment) in the case of U&G; further, user and system characteristics interact to produce flow experiences or gratifying outcomes. The reader may also wish to investigate discipline specific theories depending on the type of technology they wish to study. For instance, research on engagement with digital health interventions (DHIs) prominently features behavior change theories (Michie & Johnston, 2012; Perski et al., 2017), and education researchers may adopt Self-determination Theory (Deci & Ryan, 2008) to explain people's motivations for engaging in digital learning environments (Wiebe & Sharek, 2016). The theory pool is deep, but we will have to be content to skim the surface in the following sections.

Flow Theory

Flow Theory, also known as the Theory of Optimal Experiences. is among the most cited theories in relation to user engagement (Doherty & Doherty, 2019). Founder Mihaly Csikszentmihalyi (1990) observed that activities like rock climbing, reading, creating art, and meditating induced a state of flow, a condition "in which people are so involved in an activity that nothing else seems to matter; the experience itself is so enjoyable that people will do it even at great cost, for the sheer sake of doing it" (Csikszentmihaly, 1990, p. 4). Many studies emphasize the focused attention aspect of flow, but it is much more than absorption. Flow Theory stresses pleasurable experiences where people have clear goals about what they want to accomplish, perceive they are in control during the interaction, and receive feedback from their environment on their progress toward their goals. While focused attention is part of the flow state, intrinsic motivation, and meaning making are also critical (Csikszentmihaly, 1990).

Flow Theory was adapted and adopted in human-computer interaction research to explore users' motivations to use and responses to computer applications (e.g., email, spreadsheets) based on task and situational factors, such as in workplace settings (Finneran & Zhang, 2003; Ghani & Deshpande, 1994; Konradt & Sulz, 2001; Webster et al., 1993; Woszczynski et al., 2002). Flow theory has also been used to model engagement in digital gaming and learning environments (Chapman et al. 2023; Özhan & Kocadere, 2020; Sharek, 2010; Sharek & Wiebe, 2011), and with other conceptual frameworks to bring a more nuanced understanding to specific contexts where engagement is taking place. For example, O'Brien and Toms (2008) analyzed the attributes of Flow Theory, such as focused attention, intrinsic motivation, goal-directedness, etc., in parallel with elements of Play Theory,[2] Aesthetic Theory,[3] and Information Interaction[4] to develop the Process Model of User Engagement (see "Models" below).

Flow Theory's seven main attributes: focused attention, feedback, control, goal-directedness, activity-orientation, intrinsic motivation, and the creation of meaning (Csikszentmihalyi, 1990) are part of engaging experiences (Chapman, 1997; Jacques, 1996; O'Brien & Toms, 2008). However, I would argue that some of Flow Theories attributes have been lost in the study of engagement today.

Evaluating user engagement in online spaces uses metrics related to frequency and duration of use as proxies for user engagement. These are indicators that users may be *attending* to online platforms often and for long periods of time. However, other important aspects of the experience, like users' goals, sense of agency or intrinsic motivation, are not discernible from these behaviors (O'Brien et al., 2022); i.e., flow is not the same as usage (Chen et al., 2019; Perski et al., 2017). Csikszentmihalyi also advocated for striking a balance between "the challenges perceived in a given situation and the skills a person brings to it" (Csikszentmihalyi, 1988, p. 30); situations that fail to achieve this may lead to apathy, "a sphere of stagnation and attentional diffusion" (Nakamura & Csikszentmihalyi, 2002, p. 95). This implies that staying in flow is *not mindless but mindful* and involves cognitive effort. Yet, recent studies have shown that users of online social media and search systems increasingly associate user engagement with ease of use and limited expenditure of cognitive effort (Kang & Lou, 2022; O'Brien et al., 2020a, 2020b).

---

[2] Play is an "engaging and deliberate activity" that requires "effort and commitment" (Rieber, 1996, p. 45), emphasizing enjoyment and self-regulation, which is connected to qualities of optimal experience. Theories of Play have been applied to news reading (Stephenson, 1967) and browsing (Toms, 2002).

[3] Aesthetics is the visual appearance of the interface as it conforms to design principles (i.e. symmetry, balance, emphasis, harmony, proportion, rhythm, and unity) (Beardsley, 1982). Yet, it is also more than this. Beardsley's philosophy of Aesthetic Experiences focused on unity or wholeness of experience, focused attention/object directedness, active discovery, affect, and intrinsic motivation.

[4] Information Interaction is the integrated process of locating information (via querying and browsing), within the parameters of a context or situated action, facilitated by previous experience with the information system (Toms, 2002).

Thus, while engagement is consistently grounded in the literature of Flow Theory, we are increasingly moving away from some of its central tenets *in practice*.

Uses and Gratifications Theory

Another theory that is used frequently in engagement research is Uses and Gratifications (U&G). U&G explores why people turn to mass media to fulfill social and psychological needs and what motivates media behavior (Katz et al., 1973; LaRose & Eastin, 2004; Ruggiero, 2000). Motivations may include entertainment (e.g., escape, relaxation), habit (e.g., routine), personal identity (e.g., affirming beliefs, attitudes and values, identifying with others), social utility (e.g., finding belong, carrying out social roles, seeking status, and relationship and reputation building), and information (e.g., seeking information to satisfy curiosity or interest or to make decisions) (LaRose & Eastin, 2004; O'Brien et al., 2014; Ruggiero, 2000). Early work in U&G focused on identifying and describing people's motives for using traditional media like newspapers and television (Ruggiero, 2000). The advent of the Internet and new media, e.g., online news, entertainment streaming services, email, instant messaging, video conferencing, social media, etc., has led to new applications (Diddi & LaRose, 2006), including the study of user engagement.

McCay-Peet and Quan-Haase's (2016) model of social media engagement draws specifically on social media users' social and information motivations and how these are connected to identity construction in social media platforms. The model also links positive emotional experiences and digital affordances to social media activity and participation. McCay-Peet and Quan-Haase underscored the importance of social context in their model, which influences people's self-presentation (e.g., personal vs. professional) and gratifications sought, and guides engagement; for example, the norms and risks related to information sharing may encourage or curtail the use of some social media platform features.

This resonated with later work by Meng and Leung (2021) who found positive associations between gratifications sought and engagement behaviors on TikTok. TikTok engagement was defined as: (1) contribution behaviors, ranging from passive (watching videos) to active (like, forward, follow, comment); (2) enhancement activities, such as modifying existing content with music, special effects or subtitles; and (3) creation behaviors, e.g., making videos, streaming live video, interacting with other creators by producing similar videos, and sending private and real-time comments to creators. Identified gratifications included escape, fashion, entertainment, information seeking, money making, and sociability seeking. Money making was a unique finding of the study, while the need for sociability was limited. These findings demonstrated the applicability of McCay-Peet and Quan-Hasse's model of social media engagement (which they applied to understanding digital humanists' use of Twitter) to emerging platforms, like TikTok.

But it also makes room for appreciating the uniqueness of TikTok and people's motivations for using it, and the evolution from content consumption to creation and the rise of influencer culture.[5]

In addition to social media, streaming media, e.g., Netflix, AppleTV+, Amazon Prime, has increased in popularity over the past several years, with a reported 99% of United States households subscribing to at least one streaming provider. Netflix is leading the pack with over 260 million subscribers worldwide and the most highly rated user interface (Durrani, 2024). Emphasis on user experience highlights the value of recommender systems that curate content for users,[6] and the need to understand users' motivations for using streaming services and response to recommendations. For instance, Oh et al. 's (2022) examination of motivational differences between personalized and serendipitous movie content recommendations showed that, while serendipitous recommendations may be more enjoyable for users seeking entertainment, they may require more mental effort for users seeking information, making the system appear less functional (Oh et al., 2022). This study showed that engagement is instigated by different motivations (i.e., information, entertainment), and that recommendations systems should be aligned with user motivations.

Motivation has long been considered a central attribute of engagement in digital environments (Jacques, 1996; O'Brien, 2010; Webster & Ho, 1997). U&G focuses on individual media use, but also considers structure (i.e., how individuals relate to media and social systems), media and communication activities, and outcomes of these activities (Rubin, 1986, p. 286) making it a useful framework for understanding engagement. According to U&G, new media give rise to new patterns of communication, choice, and user control (Picone, 2007; Ruggiero, 2000), and this lens can help us to understand the mechanisms of digital engagement.

One critique of U&G is that it assumes media audiences are active and conscious of their needs, motivations, and selections (Chua et al., 2012; Rubin, 1986; Ruggiero, 2000). Communications scholars have asserted that people may not actively select media when faced with information overload (LaRose & Eastin, 2004, p. 195), be mindful of the gratifications they receive from media (Lee & Ma, 2012), nor satisfy the gratifications they seek to fulfil (Ku et al., 2013). These limitations bear consideration in today's digital ecosystem where people spend time engaging with algorithms and cultivating "the self" in lieu of interacting with media content itself (Bhandari & Bimo, 2022).

---

[5] For influencers, increased engagement has financial benefits, such as such as generating income from TikTok's Creator Fund, securing sponsorship deals with brands and companies, participating in affiliate marketing, and receiving virtual tokens or "tips" from followers on TikTok and other social media platforms (Abidin, 2020; Bauman & Rivers, 2023; Haenlein et al., 2020; Jaipong, 2023).

[6] Quite literally. The industry is currently valued at $544 billion (Durrani, 2024).

2.2 Creating Connections: Models of User Engagement

Several models of user engagement have been proposed to understand or explain user engagement (more information on models of user engagement can be found in O'Brien (2016) and Doherty and Doherty (2019)). Some models emphasize micro processes or "individual episodes of interaction," while others examine macro processes that incorporate structural, temporal, and contextual factors. Some models are conceptual in nature and show engagement as a process or a series of stages, or how engagement might be related to other concepts in the specific use context; other models use statistical techniques like structural equation modeling to mathematically test relationships between engagement and other variables.

This section does not offer a comprehensive list of all models used in association with user engagement but focuses on specific examples of a micro model (Process Model of User Engagement), a measurement model (Four-Factor Model of Media Engagement) and a macro model (Human-Artificial Intelligence Interaction (HAII) Framework). This section's goal is to show different ways that engagement has been modeled and how these models have been used by the original authors and others over time to enhance our understanding of user engagement.

2.3 Micro Model Example: The Process Model of User Engagement

As part of my dissertation research, I developed the Process Model of User Engagement (O'Brien & Toms, 2008). This would best be described as a conceptual, stage-based, micro model because it attempted to show how engagement would unfold for a technology user. The Process Model was inspired by an interdisciplinary literature review and critical incident interviews with online learners, shoppers, searchers and gamers. It consists of four stages: a point of engagement, period of sustained engagement, disengagement and re-engagement (Figure 2.1). Different attributes of engagement (e.g., attention, motivation, interest) ebb and flow throughout the stages, fostering continued or renewed engagement, or bringing the engagement to an end (O'Brien, 2008; O'Brien & Toms, 2008). While not a stage, non-engagement was also articulated by people I interviewed. This occurred for many reasons (e.g., lack of time or interest in the activity) but the point here is that engagement was not part of every computer-mediated interaction (and doesn't have to be).

Engagement begins with a point of engagement, whereby users' attention or interest is piqued by aesthetic or informational components of a digital system; motivation is also a key driver at this stage. Interest and attention persist during period of engagement. During this stage, novel content and system affordances, including user control, feedback, and appropriate levels of challenge, encourage engagement to continue. Users disengage when

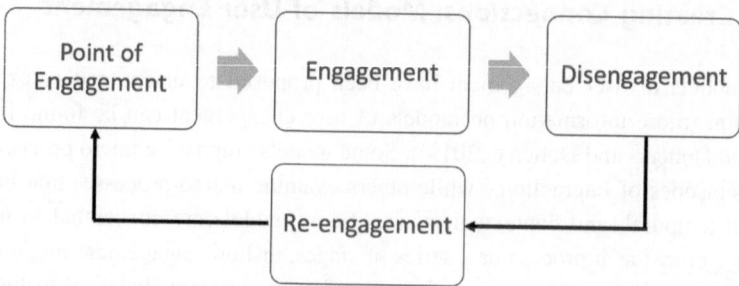

Fig. 2.1 Process model of user engagement

they have satisfied a goal or intention for using the system, but they may also discontinue use if they encounter usability issues or become distracted by external elements, e.g., an email or text notification; disengagement does not have to be a negative experience or something to avoid. Finally, re-engagement may occur immediately or in future as users seek to continue with an activity or return to an application they have enjoyed using in the past.

I returned to the Process Model in recent work with colleagues to examine disengagement in a more nuanced way (O'Brien et al., 2022). Specifically, we challenged engagement and disengagement as binary states. While disengagement may indicate the end of an activity, it can also mean a pause or a transition to another related activity or application. We proposed a series of engagements (Engagement—Disengagement—Reengagement) with different online and offline resources around a primary task. This was inspired by Paul's (2011) concept of Theorycrafting, World of Warcraft players' complimentary engagement with out-of-game resources, e.g., books, videos, player forums, to enhance gameplay. Finally, we also presented the Process Model as nested cycles of micro engagements that could occur over time, such as in online learning environments, whereby users build on past experiences and use multiple tools, to achieve context specific outcomes, such as learning.

2.4 Application of the Process Model of User Engagement

Over time, models are ideally operationalized or tested empirically in research studies. This might involve using a model as a framework to inform study design (*guiding*), comparing a model to research findings to identify areas of convergence and divergence (*checking*), and situating study findings with respect to past research and practice (*sense making*). This section explores these three avenues for using models with the Process Model of User Engagement as exemplar.

Model as Guide

Xiao et al. (2022) drew upon the Process Model of User Engagement in their examination of gamification and the Internet of Things. They constructed an analytical engagement framework consisting of three axes to support their systematic literature review: the Stage Axis, the Engagement Scale Axis, and the Cognitive-Behavior Outcome Axis. The Stage Axis drew upon the Process Model and contained non-engagement, the point of engagement, sustained engagement, and prolonged engagement; disengagement and re-engagement were not explicitly featured. Second, the Engagement Scale Axis displayed individual or single-user engagement, multi-user (e.g., specific group, community), and public engagement. Lastly, the Cognitive-Behavior Outcome Axis looked at psychological mechanisms: attentional, motivational, attitudinal, and behavioral engagement. The axes provided a means to evaluate the literature and assess the extent of empirical work on the engagement process, intended users, and outcomes. Regarding the Stage Axis, the authors noted that sustained engagement was the most prominent focus of the literature they reviewed, followed by the point of engagement and long-term engagement, with limited attention to non-engagement. They concluded that more emphasis is placed on engagement as a positive experience, leaving disengagement an "unexploited space in the field" (Xiao et al., 2022, p. 1121), and pointing to future research directions.

Another example of using the Process Model as a guide is that of Simblett et al. (2018). They conducted a systematic review of barriers and facilitators of using remote measuring technology (RMT) for health management. They used their findings to propose a new model that expanded on the first stage of the Process Model. Specifically, the point of engagement—deciding whether to engage in a health intervention—consisted of five key factors: a person's health status, usability of the intervention, convenience/accessibility of the intervention, the perceived utility of engagement (i.e., rewards vs. benefits), and personal motivation. Each of these five factors was mapped to a suite of barriers and facilitators. For example, the lack of intrinsic motivation was a barrier to personal motivation, while the presence of clinicians could act as both a barrier and a facilitator. In this example, the Process Model provided a structure within which to dive more deeply into why people engage with RMT's in the first place, and to understand the factors that were contributing to or deterring use.

Model as Check

Burns et al. (2020) conducted interviews with individuals and groups recruited from a global workplace challenge to walk 10,000 steps per day; participants used different activity-tracking technologies, e.g. pedometers, Fitbits, that they accessed through their smartphones or wearables like watches. The authors found that the four-stage Process Model of User Engagement resonated with their data, but added two additional stages, "self-management" and "limited engagement." Self-management was "a stage where users had completely disengaged from their technology" but "were still engaged with their health activity" (Burns et al., 2020, p. 6). Limited engagement was present in the group study findings only and occurred "when users had minimal interaction with their mHealth technology but engaged in the health activity to contribute to the group goals" (p. 6). While these two stages may or may not be present in non-health contexts, they are important contributions to the Process Model. First, the "self-management" stage shows that engagement with digital technologies, such as health interventions or trackers, is not the same thing as engagement with the targeted health behavior. Cole-Lewis et al. (2019) distinguish these as "Little e" and "Big E" engagement, respectively, making the point that technology use is just one aspect of health engagement. Second, the Process Model focused on individual rather than social experiences. The "limited engagement" stage adds new insights into how social dynamics might influence engagement and behaviors.

Burns et al. (2020) also noted that the engagement stages were non-linear, and that participants skipped stages depending on factors like motivation and personal accountability. In the original Process Model, I imagined that some attributes might be more salient during some stages than others. Burns et al. (2020) took a similar approach to mapping themes and attributes to each of their six stages. Despite some variability, they observed that participants' motivation to achieve goals and receive social support were consistent themes across the six stages. This mapping provides design directions for digital health challenges and related technologies.

Model as Sense Making

Lin et al. (2018) did not explicitly use the Process Model but focused on re-engagement as a stage of longitudinal use (31+ months) of a mobile physical activity tracking application. Data consisted of 115 million logged activities (e.g., number of check-ins and distinct activities per week) from over a million users and was used to compare initial and re-engagement patterns. The researchers found that over 75% of users re-engaged with the app despite long periods of inactivity, demonstrating that user engagement patterns changed over time with user needs and goals. They described the "multiple lives of user engagement," where users stopped using apps when they reached their goals, and then re-engaged when new goals were formed. These findings disrupt notions of who is considered a continuing user. The authors pointed out that many apps used notifications to try to re-engage users, but these did not always work. A larger percentage of users returned to the app after long absences (e.g., 90 days) and this renewed use was "not a continuation of the previous usage patterns, but it looks as if they are using the app for the first time" (Lin et al., 2018, p. 3). Although users re-engaged as they set new goals, they returned primarily due to performance setbacks, i.e., previous activity, sleep or weight loss goals were lost, that made app use necessary again.

2.5   Example of Measurement Models: Four Factor Model of Interactive Media

Measurement models attempt to mathematically test the relationship between theoretical constructs. A good example of a measurement model is the Four Factor Model of Interactive Media (Oh et al., 2018). The proposed conceptual model has four components: (1) *Physical interaction* with the interface, "the amount of observable activity of users with the interface" (p. 742); (2) *Interface assessment*, "users' initial evaluation of the interface" (p. 743); (3) *Absorption*, "where the individual is consciously involved in an interaction, and more specifically with the content of the interaction, with almost complete attentional focus on the mediated environment" (p. 744); and (4) *Digital outreach*, described as "a heightened phase of engagement which is marked by several behavioral (action-filled) indicators" (p. 744), e.g., bookmarking or sharing content. The authors hypothesized that users' physical interactions and assessment of the interface would lead to absorption, which would result in digital outreach.

To test the conceptual model, the researchers gathered data from two experimental lab studies with undergraduate students. Study 1 participants interacted with six prototype websites of a magazine story featuring different interactive affordances, e.g., click, mouseover, drag, and slide. Study 2 presented eight websites that utilized combinations of interactive techniques (e.g., click and slide) and contained either static or 3D carousel images.

Confirmatory Factor Analysis (CFA) and Structural Equation Modeling were used to test the conceptual model. Physical interaction was operationalized based on participants' interactions with and time spent on interface hotspots, while other components of the model were measured with self-report questions. Results indicated good reliability and validity of the model and the four factors constituting it. A major contribution of this research was the combination of actual behaviors and self-reports into one model. In addition, Oh et al. (2018) considered how content and interface affordances engaged users, and that, once absorbed in the interaction, users performed further actions to reinforce their media participation.

In future work, Oh and Kang (2021) used the four-factor model in a study with "smart wearables," or applications that can collect user data and be worn on the body. They conducted an online survey of 450+ current users of smartwatches and fitness trackers. The survey contained questions about physical interactions, interface assessment, absorption and digital outreach, and attitudes toward the devices and intentions to continue using them. Factor analysis supported the original four factors of Oh et al.'s (2018) model, but the interaction pathways between variables were different. Specifically, physical interactions (e.g., checking and tapping the device, using voice commands) predicted interface assessment (e.g., as easy to use), which then predicted cognitive absorption and enjoyment, leading to outreach (i.e., recommending the device to others through in person and social networks). They also observed a strong, positive correlation between user engagement and their attitudes toward the devices and intentions to continue using them.

2.6   Example of Macro Model: Human-Artificial Intelligence Interaction (HAII) Framework

Sundar (2020) focused on the agentic relationship between humans and technologies in the Human-Artificial Intelligence Interaction (HAII) Framework. The author drew from scholarship that placed human-technology relationships on a spectrum of passive (mainly human-driven) to active (mainly machine driven), reflecting on the proliferation of technologies that "proactively direct our attention with notifications and dictate our behaviors with suggestions, e.g., smartwatches that urge us to get up and walk" (Sundar, 2020, p. 76). Sundar looked at the influence of Artificial Intelligence (AI) on the content we interact with across different media to enhance the Theory of Interactive Media Effects (TIME) (Sundar et al., 2015) with Human-AI Interaction (HAII).

The HAII-TIME model consists of three main components: (1) Predictors (e.g., attributes of the algorithm based on perceptions or cues, and affordances of the AI medium based on actions or experiences), (2) Mediators (e.g., cognitive heuristics, human-machine agency, sustained interaction), and (3) Outcomes (perceptions and engagement with the AI medium, which determines trust in and user experience with AI). Sundar indicated that empirical work is needed to investigate the ways in which humans and machines "co-create reality," but that the model can prompt consideration of the "social and psychological consequences of emerging communications technologies" (Sundar, 2020, p. 84).

This model will be particularly useful as artificial intelligence technologies continue to be embedded in everyday life, including social media. Kang and Lou (2022), for example, interviewed 25 young adult TikTok users to explore the relationship between user and machine agency, and how this facilitates user engagement, i.e., consumption, creation and sharing behaviors. User agency was defined as user activity (Sundar, 2008), and machine agency was examined according to the "agency enhancing affordances" of social media, including options for customization, commenting, sharing, liking, i.e., digital outreach (Oh & Kang, 2021; Oh et al., 2018). Results indicated that interviewees were guided by TikTok's "For You" page because it offered personalization and convenience and required limited cognitive effort. They did, however, expend effort to understand how the algorithms produced recommendations by, for example, creating multiple accounts until content was deemed interesting and relevant. Cognitive effort was also a factor in content creation because users needed to learn to use video editing tools to make sophisticated videos.

Kang and Lou considered users' experiences with agency on the platform, observing that although they "generally exercise limited user agency, they still aspire to secure user agency" (Kang & Lou, 2022, p. 6). Interviewees described TikTok as engaging and addictive due to the "endless content feed tailored to their interests" (Kang & Lou, 2022, p. 7). The findings highlighted the role of desirable uncertainty, where participants described some unpredictability about what content they would be shown next, yet also trust and anticipation that the recommendations would be of interest. This study also exemplified elements of the HAII Framework in that the FYP predicted mediating variables, including the users' sense of agency, interactions (e.g., scrolling, creating) and investment of cognitive effort; this led to outcomes related to users' engagement with TikTok, perceptions about how it worked, and trust in the platform.

Chapter Summary

This chapter provided an overview of how user engagement has been conceptualized. Two theoretical frameworks used to study engagement, Flow Theory and Uses and Gratifications Theory, were described. These theories highlight specific attributes that are used to define user engagement, e.g., focused attention, interest, and motivation. A selection of models of engagement were presented to illustrate different kinds of models (micro, measurement, macro) and what can be learned from them.

Engagement is pluralistic in the sense that different theoretical frameworks and models can be used to support the design and evaluation of engagement research and make sense of digital experiences. This should not be viewed as a detriment. The strength of engagement research is its interdisciplinarity and the diverse contexts in which it is studied.

This is not to say, however, that researchers should do away with theory. Rather, scholars should explicate how they are defining engagement in their work and ground themselves in relevant theories and models appropriate to their setting, the user group of interest, and the technology they are examining. Acknowledging the rich, multifaceted history of the concept is essential for building new knowledge and testing how theory works in practice. It also underscores that engagement is more than a behavioral metric. Taking time to appreciate and consider its emotional and cognitive elements and how these come to bear in user experience leads to more multifaceted and grounded research.

References

Abidin, C. (2020). Mapping internet celebrity on TikTok: Exploring attention economies and visibility labours. *Cultural Science Journal, 12*(1), 77–103. https://doi.org/10.5334/csci.140

Azevedo, R. (2015). Defining and measuring engagement and learning in science: Conceptual, theoretical, methodological, and analytical issues. *Educational Psychologist, 50*(1), 84–94. https://doi.org/10.1080/00461520.2015.1004069

Bates, M. J. (2005). An introduction to metatheories, theories and models. In K. E. Fisher, S. Erdelez, & L. E. F. McKechnie (Eds.), *Theories of information behavior* (pp. 1–24). ASIS&T.

Bauman, S., & Rivers, I. (2023). Social media and forms of connectedness. In S. Bauman & I. Rivers (Eds.), *Mental health in the digital age* (pp. 59–83). Springer International Publishing. https://doi.org/10.1007/978-3-031-32122-1_4

Beardsely, M. (1982). *The aesthetic point of view: selected essays.* Cornell University Press.

Bhandari, A., & Bimo, S. (2022). Why's everyone on TikTok Now? The algorithmized self and the future of self-making on social media. *Social Media and Society, 8*(1), 205630512210862–205630512210862. https://doi.org/10.1177/20563051221086241

Burns, K., Nicholas, R., Beatson, A., Chamorro-Koc, M., Blackler, A., & Gottlieb, U. (2020). Identifying mobile health engagement stages: Interviews and observations for developing brief message content. *Journal of Medical Internet Research, 22*(9), e15307. https://doi.org/10.2196/15307

Chapman, J. R., Kohler, T. B., Rich, P. J., & Trego, A. (2023). Maybe we've got it wrong. An experimental evaluation of self-determination and flow theory in gamification. *Journal of Research on Technology in Education*, 1–20. https://doi.org/10.1080/15391523.2023.2242981

Chapman, P. (1997). *Models of engagement: Intrinsically motivated interaction with multimedia learning software.* [Master's Thesis]. University of Waterloo.

Chen, A. T., Wu, S., Tomasino, K. N., Lattie, E. G., & Mohr, D. C. (2019). A multi-faceted approach to characterizing user behavior and experience in a digital mental health intervention. *Journal of Biomedical Informatics, 94*, 103187. https://doi.org/10.1016/j.jbi.2019.103187

Chua, A. Y. K., Goh, D. H., & Lee, C. S. (2012). Mobile content contribution and retrieval: An exploratory study using the uses and gratifications paradigm. *Information Processing and Management, 48*(1), 13–22.

Cole-Lewis, H., Ezeanochie, N., & Turgiss, J. (2019). Understanding health behavior technology engagement: Pathway to measuring digital behavior change interventions. *JMIR Formative Research, 3*(4), e14052. https://doi.org/10.2196/14052

Cooksey, R., & McDonald, G. (2019). *Surviving and thriving in postgraduate research.* Springer.https://doi.org/10.1007/978-981-13-7747-1

Creswell, J. W. (2014). *Research design: Qualitative, quantitative, and mixed methods approaches* (4th Edn). SAGE Publication.

Csikszentmihalyi, M. (1988). The flow experience and its significance for human psychology. In I. S. Csikszentmihalyi & M. Csikszentmihalyi (Eds.), *Optimal experience: Psychological studies of flow in consciousness* (pp. 15–35). Cambridge University Press. https://doi.org/10.1017/CBO9780511621956.002

Csikszentmihalyi, M. (1990). *The psychology of optimal experience* (Vol. 1). Harper & Row.

Cunningham, T., Pandey, S., Sigerson, L., Stray, J., Allen, J., Barrilleaux, B., Iyer, R., Milli, S., Kothari, M., & Rezaei, B. (2024). *What we know about using non-engagement signals in content ranking* (arXiv:2402.06831). arXiv. https://doi.org/10.48550/arXiv.2402.06831

Deci, E. L., & Ryan, R. M. (2008). Self-determination theory: A macrotheory of human motivation, development, and health. *Canadian Psychology/psychologie Canadienne, 49*(3), 182.

Diddi, A., & LaRose, R. (2006). Getting hooked on news: Uses and gratifications and the formation of news habits among college students in an internet environment. *Journal of Broadcasting and Electronic Media, 50*(2), 193–210. https://doi.org/10.1207/s15506878jobem5002_2

Doherty, K., & Doherty, G. (2019). Engagement in HCI: Conception, theory and measurement. *ACM Computing Surveys, 51*(5), 1–39. https://doi.org/10.1145/3234149

Durrani, A. (2024, June 13). *2024 Media Streaming Stats You Should Know—Forbes Home.* Forbes Home. https://www.forbes.com/home-improvement/internet/streaming-stats/

Fidel, R. (2012). Theoretical constructs and models in information-seeking behavior. In *Human information interaction: An ecological approach to information behavior* (pp. 49–81). MIT Press.

Finneran, C. M., & Zhang, P. (2003). A person-artefact-task (PAT) model of flow antecedents in computer-mediated environments. *International Journal of Human-Computer Studies, 59*, 475–496.

Ghani, J. A., & Deshpande, S. (1994). Task characteristics and the experience of optimal flow in human-computer interaction. *The Journal of Psychology, 128*(4), 381–391.

Haenlein, M., Anadol, E., Farnsworth, T., Hugo, H., Hunichen, J., & Welte, D. (2020). Navigating the new era of influencer marketing: How to be successful on Instagram, TikTok, & Co. *California Management Review, 63*(1), 5–25. https://doi.org/10.1177/0008125620958166

Jacques, R. D. (1996). *The nature of engagement and its role in hypermedia evaluation and design* [Doctoral Dissertation]. South Bank University.

Jaipong, P. (2023). Business model and strategy: A case study analysis of TikTok. *Advance Knowledge for Executives (AKE), 2*, 1–18.

Kang, H., & Lou, C. (2022). AI agency versus human agency: Understanding human–AI interactions on TikTok and their implications for user engagement. *Journal of Computer-Mediated Communication, 27*(5), zmac014. https://doi.org/10.1093/jcmc/zmac014

Katz, E., Blumler, J. G., & Gurevitch, M. (1973). Uses and gratification research. *Public Opinion Quarterly, 37*(4), 509–523. https://doi.org/10.1086/268109

Konradt, U., & Sulz, K. (2001). The experience of flow in interacting with a hypermedia learning environment. *Journal of Educational Multimedia and Hypermedia, 10*(1), 69–84.

Ku, Y.-C., Chu, T.-H., & Tseng, C.-H. (2013). Gratifications for using CMC technologies: A comparison among SNS, IM, and e-mail. *Computers in Human Behavior, 29*(1), 226–234.

LaRose, R., & Eastin, M. S. (2004). A social cognitive theory of internet uses and gratifications: Toward a new model of media attendance. *Journal of Broadcasting and Electronic Media, 48*(3), 358–377. https://doi.org/10.1207/s15506878jobem4803_2

Lee, S. L., & Ma, L. (2012). News sharing in social media: The effect of gratifications and prior experience. *Computers in Human Behavior, 28*(2), 331–339.

Lin, Z., Althoff, T., & Leskovec, J. (2018). I'll be back: On the multiple lives of users of a mobile activity tracking application. *Proceedings of the 2018 World Wide Web Conference on World Wide Web—WWW '18* (pp. 1501–1511). https://doi.org/10.1145/3178876.3186062

Lincoln, Y. S., & Guba, E. G. (1985). *Naturalistic inquiry.* SAGE Publication.

McCay-Peet, L., & Quan-Haase, A. (2016). A model of social media engagement: User profiles, gratifications, and experiences. In H. O'Brien & P. Cairns (Eds.), *Why engagement matters.* Springer.

Meng, K. S., & Leung, L. (2021). Factors influencing TikTok engagement behaviors in China: An examination of gratifications sought, narcissism, and the big five personality traits. *Telecommunications Policy, 45*(7), 102172. https://doi.org/10.1016/j.telpol.2021.102172

Merton, R. K. (1968). *Social theory and social structure.* The Free Press.

Michie, S., & Johnston, M. (2012). Theories and techniques of behaviour change: Developing a cumulative science of behaviour change. *Health Psychology Review, 6*(1), 1–6. https://doi.org/10.1080/17437199.2012.654964

Nakamura, J., & Csikszentmihalyi, M. (2002). The concept of flow. In *Handbook of positive psychology* (pp. 89–105). Oxford University Press.

O'Brien, H. L. (2010). The influence of hedonic and utilitarian motivations on user engagement: The case of online shopping experiences. *Interacting with Computers, 22*(5), 344–352. https://doi.org/10.1016/j.intcom.2010.04.001

O'Brien, H. L. (2016). Translating theory into methodological practice. In H. O'Brien & P. Cairns (Eds.), *Why engagement matters: Cross-disciplinary perspectives of user engagement in digital media* (pp. 27–52). Springer Cham.

O'Brien, H. L., & Toms, E. G. (2008). What is user engagement? A conceptual framework for defining user engagement with technology. *Journal of the American Society for Information Science and Technology, 59*(6), 938–955. https://doi.org/10.1002/asi.20801

O'Brien, H. L., Arguello, J., & Capra, R. (2020a). An empirical study of interest, task complexity, and search behaviour on user engagement. *Information Processing and Management, 57*(3), 102226.

O'Brien, H. L., Morton, E., Kampen, A., Barnes, S. J., & Michalak, E. E. (2020b). Beyond clicks and downloads: A call for a more comprehensive approach to measuring mobile-health app engagement. *Bjpsych Open, 6*(5), e86. https://doi.org/10.1192/bjo.2020.72

O'Brien, H. L., Roll, I., Kampen, A., & Davoudi, N. (2022). Rethinking (Dis)engagement in human-computer interaction. *Computers in Human Behavior, 128*, 107109. https://doi.org/10.1016/j.chb.2021.107109

O'Brien, H. L, Freund, L., & Westman, S. (2014). *What motivates the online news browser? News item selection in a social information seeking scenario* [Text]. Professor T.D. Wilson. https://informationr.net/ir/19-3/paper634.html

O'Brien, H. L. (2008). *Defining and measuring engagement in user experiences with technology* [Doctoral Dissertation]. Dalhousie University.

Oh, J., & Kang, H. (2021). User engagement with smart wearables: Four defining factors and a process model. *Mobile Media and Communication, 9*(2), 314–335. https://doi.org/10.1177/2050157920958440

Oh, J., Bellur, S., & Sundar, S. S. (2018). Clicking, assessing, immersing, and sharing: An empirical model of user engagement with interactive media. *Communication Research, 45*(5), 737–763. https://doi.org/10.1177/0093650215600493

Oh, J., Sudarshan, S., Lee, J. A., & Yu, N. (2022). Serendipity enhances user engagement and sociality perception: The combinatory effect of serendipitous movie suggestions and user motivations. *Behaviour and Information Technology, 41*(11), 2324–2341. https://doi.org/10.1080/0144929X.2021.1921027

Özhan, ŞÇ., & Kocadere, S. (2020). The effects of flow, emotional engagement, and motivation on success in a gamified online learning environment. *Journal of Educational Computing Research, 57*(8), 2006–2031.

Paul, C. A. (2011). Optimizing play: How theorycraft changes gameplay and design. *Game Studies, 11*(2). https://gamestudies.org/1102/articles/paul

Perski, O., Blandford, A., West, R., & Michie, S. (2017). Conceptualising engagement with digital behaviour change interventions: A systematic review using principles from critical interpretive synthesis. *Translational Behavioral Medicine, 7*(2), 254–267. https://doi.org/10.1007/s13142-016-0453-1

Pickard, A. J. (2013). Major research paradigms. In *Research Methods in Information* (2nd Ed., pp. 5–24). Neal-Schuman.

Picone, I. (2007). Conceptualising online news use. *Observatorio Journal, 3*(1), 93–114.

Rieber, L. P. (1996). Seriously considering play: Designing interactive learning environments based on blending microworlds, simulations, and games. *Educational Technology Research and Development, 44*(2), 45–58. https://doi.org/10.1007/BF02300540

Rubin, A. M. (1986). Uses, gratifications, and media effects research. In J. Bryant & D. Zillmann (Eds.), *Perspectives on media effects* (pp. 281–301). Lawrence Erlbaum Associates.

Ruggiero, T. E. (2000). Uses and gratifications theory in the 21st century. *Mass Communication and Society, 3*(1), 3–37. https://doi.org/10.1207/S15327825MCS0301_02

Sharek, D., & Wiebe, E. (2011). Using flow theory to design video games as experimental stimuli. *Proceedings of the Human Factors and Ergonomics Society Annual Meeting, 55*, 1520–1524.

Sharek, D. (2010). *The influence of flow in the measure of engagement.* [Master's Thesis, North Carolina State University]. http://www.lib.ncsu.edu/resolver/1840.16/1712

Simblett, S., Greer, B., Matcham, F., Curtis, H., Polhemus, A., Ferrão, J., Gamble, P., & Wykes, T. (2018). Barriers to and facilitators of engagement with remote measurement technology for managing health: Systematic review and content analysis of findings. *Journal of Medical Internet Research, 20*(7). https://www.proquest.com/scholarly-journals/barriers-facilitators-engagement-with-remote/docview/2512779907/se-2

Stephenson, W. (1967). Play theory. In *The play theory of mass communication* (pp. 45–65). University of Chicago Press.

Sundar, S. S. (2020). Rise of machine agency: A framework for studying the psychology of human–AI interaction (HAII). *Journal of Computer-Mediated Communication, 25*(1), 74–88. https://doi.org/10.1093/jcmc/zmz026

Sundar, S. S., Jia, H., Waddell, T. F., & Huang, Y. (2015). Toward a theory of interactive media effects (TIME): Four models for explaining how interface features affect user psychology. In *The handbook of the psychology of communication technology* (pp. 47–86). Wiley Blackwell. https://doi.org/10.1002/9781118426456.ch3

Sundar, S. S. (2008). Self as source: Agency and customization in interactive media. In *Mediated interpersonal communication* (Vol. 9780203926864, pp. 58–74). Routledge Taylor & Francis Group. https://doi.org/10.4324/9780203926864

Toms, E. G. (2002). Information interaction: Providing a framework for information architecture. *Journal of the American Society for Information Science and Technology, 53*(10), 855–862. https://doi.org/10.1002/asi.10094

Webster, J., & Ho, H. (1997). Audience engagement in multimedia presentations. *ACM SIGMIS Database: the DATABASE for Advances in Information Systems, 28*(2), 63–77. https://doi.org/10.1145/264701.264706

Webster, J., Trevino, L. K., & Ryan, L. (1993). The dimensionality and correlates of flow in human-computer interactions. *Computers in Human Behavior, 9*, 411–426.

Wiebe, E., & Sharek, D. (2016). ELearning. In H. O'Brien (Ed.), *Why engagement matters: Cross-disciplinary perspectives of user engagement in digital media* (pp. 53–79).

Woszczynski, A. B., Roth, P. L., & Segars, A. H. (2002). Exploring the theoretical foundations of playfulness in computer interactions. *Computers in Human Behavior, 18*, 369–388.

Xiao, R., Wu, Z., & Hamari, J. (2022). Internet-of-gamification: A review of literature on IoT-enabled gamification for user engagement. *International Journal of Human-Computer Interaction, 38*(12), 1113–1137. https://doi.org/10.1080/10447318.2021.1990517

User Engagement with Interactive Information Systems

Many factors contribute to users' experiences with interactive information systems. People, information and technology are the "necessary ingredients" in information research and practice, and their interactions produce changes in humans (e.g., acquiring knowledge, learning) and their use of information objects over time (Marchionini, 2008). Many macro models of information interaction—and indeed user engagement[1]—demonstrate the many qualities of people, technology and information that might come to bear on user experience.

People vary in developmental stage and life experience. They have different cultural and language backgrounds, physical and cognitive abilities, skill and comfort levels with digital technology, and knowledge of assorted topics. They bring these individual differences into their interactions with technologies, using diverse devices (smartphones, tablet computers, wearables) for a variety of purposes (e.g., information, entertainment, staying connected with other people). Information systems may be of different types (e.g., search engines, academic databases, social media) and allow people to interact with information through numerous features (e.g., a search bar, menu options) and affordances (e.g.,

---

[1] There are several models of engagement with digital health interventions (DHIs) that include the role of the user, use context, information content, and system design in bringing about attitude or behavior change. These models include the Model of Internet Intervention (Ritterband et al., 2009), Model of User Engagement in Online Interventions (Short et al., 2015) and the Conceptual Framework of Direct and Indirect Influences on Engagement with Digital Behavior Change Interventions (DBCI) (Perski et al., 2017). Though situated in health contexts, these are applicable to other settings because they suggest that the environment and qualities of users determine engagement with a DHI and that the success of the intervention is shaped by attributes related to DHI design, namely content and how it is delivered.

© The Author(s), under exclusive license to Springer Nature Switzerland AG 2025
H. O'Brien, *User Engagement Research and Practice*, Synthesis Lectures on Information Concepts, Retrieval, and Services, https://doi.org/10.1007/978-3-031-80916-3_3

clickable links). Information may be on a specific subject and packaged in a particular language, format, or presentation style.

The complexity of information interactions is captured in many information science models. Toms et al. (2004), for example, depict the qualities of people, the technology medium, and information resources, and embed these in an environment or context.[2] Context may include the virtual or physical space, home, organizational or workplace culture and all its norms, routines, constraints, and available resources; context informs people's information needs and the tasks they attempt to carry out with an information system (Byström & Hansen, 2005, p. 1052). Another feature of Toms' et al.'s (2004) model is that contextually integrated interactions produce some kind of outcome that motivates the user to interact with information content and media—they are looking for something novel, interesting, credible, and so on. Engagement is one of these possible outcomes.

The question, then, is how do we bring about an *engaging* outcome? What are the "key ingredients" for engagement to take place? There is no magic formula to consistently guarantee this, nor would we necessarily want to.[3] However, over the past decades, researchers have zeroed in on qualities of people, information and technologies that might lead to engagement. In an earlier publication, we provided an overview of these findings according to:

- User characteristics, such as personality, gender, age, technology experience, domain knowledge, self-efficacy, and personal preferences.
- Content characteristics, including interestingness, sentiment and polarity, quality, evaluations of the content creator, and how content is motivated and framed.
- Technology characteristics, which can be further delineated as:
  - Aesthetics, including overall visual appeal and visual saliency of interface features; olfactory, auditory and visual cues that trigger sensory experiences.
  - Interactivity, or the functionality and the direct manipulation of interface features, e.g., clicking, zooming, dragging, animation; tactile feedback, and capacity for social interaction.
  - Media, or the use and quality of text, video and audio formats (O'Brien & McKay, 2018).

---

[2] Context has been defined in many ways in and beyond information science. Case and Given (2016) define it as "the particular combination of person and situation that serve[s] to frame an investigation" of information behavior (p. 14), while McCreadie and Rice (1999) distinguish between a situation, "the particular set of circumstances from which a need for information arises," from context, "the larger picture in which the potential user operates…the information system is developed and operates, and potential information exists"(p. 58). Harari and Gosling (2023) suggest that context can be temporal, physical, geographical, behavioral, digital, developmental and personal.

[3] In a more recent publication, we (O'Brien et al., 2022) argue that disengagement has a vital and agentic role to play in user experience.

There were a lot of dependencies in how these factors contribute to engagement. For instance, a study by Vail et al. (2014) demonstrated gender differences in students' interactions with intelligent tutoring systems, but these were dependent on whether students interacted with a human or computer-based agent and the nature of the feedback provided to learners (affective, cognitive, mixed). In other words, we cannot conclude that differences in people (in this case, gender) singularly lead to engagement outcomes; we must consider how individual differences interact with content (in this instance, feedback that focuses on topical versus emotional support) and the system itself (i.e., human and non-human tutors). It is too simplistic to say that any one user, information or technology characteristic precipitates user engagement. Rather, an engaging outcome is a constellation of factors interacting and unfolding over time.

In addition to considering how qualities of people, technologies and content interact, we must consider that studying experience at the macro level is not feasible in a single research or practice setting. It is often necessary to look at micro aspects of the experience[4]. If we return to Toms' model, there will be kinds of information systems that we are interested in, and these have associated information resources and users. For instance, studying engagement with academic databases entails specific information objects (e.g., conference proceedings, journal articles) and users (e.g., students and academic staff in a particular discipline). Other information systems are more challenging to study since they attract varied user groups (e.g., social media users vary in age, gender, and cultural make up), but we tend to narrow our inquiry based on our research questions. For instance, when we ask, "how do youth with depression engage with TikTok to support their mental health?" we are looking at a specific group of people and their interactions with a particular kind of information system for a dedicated purpose.

Examining the relationships between users, information and systems in different contexts opens endless possibilities for what might foster or deter engagement in a given scenario. This chapter summarizes recent findings that highlight the unique configurations of people, information and technology (Figure 3.1) that teach us more about engaging experiences. "Tasks" are also discussed as a product of people's interactions with information and technologies.

---

[4] This might be considered a more reductionist approach. According to Talja et al. (1999), an objectified approach considers "any factors or variables that are seen to affect individuals' information-seeking behavior: socio-economic conditions, work roles, tasks, problem situations, communities and organizations with their structures and cultures, etc.," and focuses on operationalizing and measuring them. They contrast this with interpretative approaches that view context as embedded in "the holistic theoretical perspective from which the research object is conceptualized" (p. 752). However, I think there is room for both post-positivist and interpretivist worldviews to studying engagement, especially when we put different kinds of studies into conversation with each other.

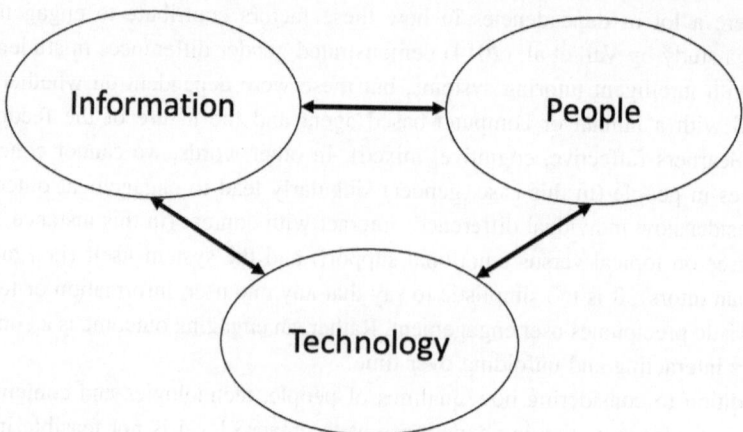

Fig. 3.1. Key ingredients of user engagement: information, people and technology

3.1   People

Information interaction studies that involve human participants tend to gather personal data from those sampled. This often includes asking questions related to demographics (e.g., age, education level), technology use (e.g., frequency of using a search engine or social media app), perceptions of technology competencies or subject expertise, and prior knowledge of topics that may be pertinent to the study. In some cases, this information is used merely to provide a description of the sample and acknowledge any sample-based limitations (e.g., participants were under the age of 35, and may not be representative of users >35 years old), or to explore whether user characteristic led to different outcomes (e.g., people who rated their subject expertise higher took less time to complete a task). Such questions are also part of engagement studies, and user characteristics may or may not be highlighted depending on the extent to which they impact the findings or are part of the research questions. This section examines select studies that have investigated *demographic* and *individual differences* with respect to engagement.

Several studies have used demographic data specifically to understand who is engaging with a technology, and how individual differences contribute to this engagement (or lack of engagement). For instance, Begany et al. (2021) found lower engagement with an open data platform amongst female identifying users, people using mobile devices to access data, older users, and those with less interest in technology; there was higher engagement amongst people with higher levels of expertise working with datasets (Begany & Gil-Garcia, 2021). Taki et al. (2017) observed that first-time mothers, those who opened weekly emails, and those who joined when their infants were younger were more highly engaged with a parenting app. Insights from these specific studies could, for instance, enhance open data literacy initiatives or outreach to new parents to encourage engagement from less engaged groups. In general, there may be utility in collecting and analyzing demographic information when the goal is to understand how to improve an information system or enhance engagement for a particular user community. However, it is imperative to acknowledge that people have intersecting identities, and that demographic data collection and reporting should subscribe to high ethical standards.

A user quality that receives a great deal of attention in information interaction research is search and domain expertise (c.f. Bailey, 2017; Wildemuth, 2004; Wildemuth et al., 2018); with some exceptions (Sundar et al., 2014) this is under explored with respect to engagement. However, Agosti et al. (2018) observed differences based on expertise in their study of engagement in the CULTURA project, a European collaboration to enhance access to digital cultural heritage collections. Focusing on two specific collections, the authors explored the experiences of non-professional users over a three-year period. This involved cataloguing user requirements and identifying the salience of specific features for defined user groups to reveal design insights. They noted that less experienced users wanted tools to support non-directed browsing, whereas professional users wanted tools for non-item searching, such as artefacts and collections of interest. Users also desired customization, including the ability to create workspaces for different projects and organize bookmarks and annotations in folders, and to integrate annotations and bookmarked content into workflows, including moving content to spaces outside of the digital library environment.

Wang et al. (2020) experimented with different degrees of social interaction that illustrated different levels of independence, presence and control in a virtual museum. Interview participants were asked to view and reflect on videos showing different social interaction modes. They noticed that collaborators in the videos appeared more engaged when they were coupled (shared, leader, and passive control conditions) and users interacted more with the environment than with collaborators in independent navigation modes. Variations in participants' reactions to the conditions showed that individual differences affected people's preferences for how they would want to interact in the virtual world; some expressed concerns about being in modes where they would have less control when collaborating with someone they did not know.

An interesting study by Arguello and Choi (2019) investigated the effects of working memory, perceptual speed and inhibitory attention control on user engagement with two, custom-built aggregated search interfaces containing web, news, image, video and shopping search results. There were no significant differences in self-reported engagement between the two interfaces, demonstrating the potential for user preferences to shape people's evaluation of their experience. However, working memory was related to dimensions of user engagement and search performance was linked to perceptual speed and inhibitory attention control. This findings suggests that engagement and performance outcomes are distinct and may be dependent on different cognitive processes.

3.2   Information

There are many aspects of information content that have been investigated with respect to engagement. This section explores research relating to genre and format, structure and paralinguistic cues, sentiment and polarity, and user comprehension and trust.

Genre and Format

Schellewald (2021) explored communicative forms or genres on TikTok through ethnographic observation. They identified six types: comedic, documentary, communal (showing friends and family), interactive (asking others to demonstrate skills), explanatory (telling others how to do something), and "meta." Meta videos borrow genre characteristics from the other formats and feature content that focuses on the app itself, i.e., "how TikTok's algorithms place content in your feed from users that have similar interests or who are in a similar life situation" (p. 1449–1450). The author called these meta videos checkpoints or "speedbumps" that "try to break with that [predominant] rhythm" of the platform, opening opportunities to become aware of one's own presence on the platform and within the flow of the For You Page (FYP).

Other studies have focused on how alternative, non-text formats affect engagement. Such formats include infographics (images that present "data or information through visual encoding") (Amit-Danhi & Shifman, 2022, p. 6x), data visualizations, video abstracts of research papers, and conversational agents. These formats may influence users' capacity to engage by affecting cognitive load (Amit-Danhi & Shifman, 2022)[5] or attracting users' attention (O'Brien & Toms, 2008), but more evidence is needed to understand if and how they are engaging. For instance, Li et al.'s (2023) study of social science video abstracts (VAs) demonstrated a disconnect between engagement and comprehension. Participants' comprehension of the VAs did not differ based on format (animation or slideshow), but they rated their engagement with animation VAs higher. There was also a weak, negative association between self-reported engagement and recall, indicating that engagement and comprehension may have been at odds.

Studies with infographics have focused on design (Comello et al., 2016) and content type (Amit-Danhi & Shifman, 2022). Comello et al. (2016) tested traditional and game-inspired infographics depicting health content. Game-inspired infographics featured either a scorecard or a progress bar to provide feedback on the users' status toward goal completion status. The authors found no differences in information processing outcomes for the two versions, but engagement was higher for the gamified infographics that used progress bars, especially amongst those not at the recommended level for the health behavior described in the infographic. This suggests that gamified design elements could motivate users who need more support in achieving a health goal. Another study by Amit-Danhi

---

[5] Dual coding theory would suggest the use of different modalities (e.g., auditory, visual and haptic) to connect sensory (bodily) and symbolic (language) systems and deepen information processing capacities (Paivio, 1991).

et al. (2022) investigated infographics with two kinds of content: informational enhancers that support information processing, and evidential enhancers that facilitate credibility and validity assessments. They sampled existing infographics posted to Facebook from the 2016 United States election and found strong, positive correlations between behavioral engagement and infographics that used scientific charts and source citations. The authors predicted that infographics with emotional cues, interactive features, and calls to action would also increase engagement, but this was not supported. This study called attention to correlations between information presentation and the extent to which people interacted with it, but does not address the relationship between information accuracy or quality and engagement.

Structure and Paralinguistic Cues

In addition to format, researchers have explored elements of documents, such as length and composition. Haider et al. (2015) examined multimodal elements of "Ted Talks" video segments, along with user ratings of the videos, to create machine learning models with different feature sets: visual and paralinguistic features (i.e., camera angles, laughter, applause); speech expression features; and visual, paralinguistic and speech expression features combined. Haider et al. (2015) emphasized that engagement with video segments may be different from engagement with the video as a whole. Indeed, user ratings of the videos did not significantly differ; people who chose to comment provided mostly positive feedback. This suggests that capturing engagement during an interaction may be different than more product-based measures.

Violot et al. (2024) investigated the length of YouTube videos according to their engagement metrics, i.e., total view count, number of likes and comments, subscriber count. They concluded that short videos (i.e., Shorts) garnered 110 times more views than the regular videos, and that, over time, there was a decline in views for regular views and an increase in attention to the short videos. However, the longer videos had more comments per view than short videos. The authors speculated this could be due to topical differences between Shorts and regular videos, but could also signal more reflective engagement on the longer videos where viewers paused rather than "rapidly swiping to the next video" (p. 8). These findings show that engagement outcomes can move beyond merely number of views to more thoughtful interactions with content.

Sentiment and Polarity

The role of sentiment in content engagement is well established. Salehabadi et al. (2022) examined Twitter conversations using a toxicity detection tool to score publicly available primary tweets and their direct replies as toxic or non-toxic. Machine learning methods were used to analyze a random sample of these Tweets. Findings indicated that toxic conversations were initiated by less identifiable sources, garnered greater participation, and were longer than non-toxic conversations, potentially because more people are drawn into these kinds of conversations. If the original Tweet was toxic, replies were significantly more likely to be toxic and, if the first reply to the original Tweet was toxic, subsequent replies were also prone to be more toxic. This study would suggest that negative content is more engaging, but a study by Bil-Jaruzelska and Monzer (2022) provides a bit more nuance. They studied Facebook posts by British political parties and their leaders ($n = 1203$) during the Brexit referendum debate (April-July 2016). They operationalized engagement as the total number of interactions a post received, including "likes," "comments," "shares," and "reactions". They found that appeals to anger, enthusiasm, and pride were strong predictors of engagement, but fear appeals had no effect. Thus, a combination of negative and positive emotions fostered engagement with political content in this study.

Edelson et al. (2021) sought to distinguish "misinformation" from "factual" news outlets by sampling 7.5 million posts and metadata from over 2500 Facebook pages related to the 2020 United States presidential election. Data was collected over a 5-month period (August 2020-January 2021). Engagement was operationalized as "number of comments, shares, and reactions, e.g., likes" (p. 445) in order to examine engagement with pages, posts, and within the overall news ecosystem. The researchers used News-Guard's "partisanship" (i.e., political leaning, bias) and "factualness" (i.e., reputation for sharing misinformation) labels to categorize news websites. Findings revealed that misinformation spread by far-right news sources garnered higher levels of engagement than non-misinformation sources. Although misinformation news sources for other political leanings saw less engagement, there was, overall, a fair amount of engagement with misinformation sources. There were fewer misinformation news sources in the total sample of websites, but these pages had more average followers; further, posts featuring misinformation saw greater engagement than non-misinformation posts. One limitation of the work was that the authors were unable to obtain impression data to appreciate the nature of the engagement, i.e., followers, sponsors, shares.

Comprehension and Trust

People's ability to understand and trust content has implications for user engagement. The relationship between engagement and comprehension may be mediated by cognitive load (Dvir et al., 2023), and the link between engagement and trust is important to investigate given recent advances in artificial intelligence applications.

Few studies focus on comprehension and its relationship to engagement (Li et al., 2023). Ghafourian et al. (2023) examined common readability measures (e.g., Flesch Kincaid Grade Level Index, Gunning's Fog Index, Flesh Reading Ease) in a study that asked people to rate the relevance, understandability, and engagement of web pages; engagement was defined as motivational value for learning about the topic. Web page readability was highly associated with user-assigned understandability values and predicted participants' engagement. Comprehension was linked to how much effort searchers expended to understand if there was a fit between their information need and the information they had on hand to address that need.

Information researchers are beginning to explore and document the impact of generative artificial intelligence on information behavior and retrieval. An exploratory study by Capra and Arguello's (2023) showed that participants who utilized a chat tool to help as they searched for information adopted it to either sketch out background information for the search task or as a question-answering tool. While varying levels of trust in generative AI tools were expressed, interviewees stated that they liked the concise answers and syntheses that were outputs of the chat tool. Another study by Robbemond et al.'s (2022) asked participants to rate the perceived credibility of statements with and without AI-assisted support, while also experimenting with the modality of AI-assisted support (text, audio, or graphical). User engagement was higher for AI-assisted support with audio, but engagement did not differ between modalities. This is crucial because some of the modalities included explanations to inform people's decision making; while this did increase the accuracy of their credibility judgements, their engagement was unaffected.

3.3 People-Information Interactions: Tasks

In information interaction research, tasks are activities performed to accomplish a goal (Vakkari, 2003) and have been classified in many ways: by type (e.g. information seeking tasks, decision tasks), goal (e.g., concrete or abstract), product (e.g., format of information sought, intended use of the information), process (e.g., one-time versus repetitive), source (e.g., self- or externally motivated), and searchers' perceptions of task ease, importance, time sensitivity, and complexity (Li & Belkin, 2008). Research in user engagement specific to tasks is limited (in comparison to task-based research in information interaction broadly) (Rzepka et al., 2019; Toms, 2019; Wildemuth et al., 2014), but some aspects of tasks, namely how engagement can be used to make tasks more palatable, and task characteristics of topic and complexity, have been investigated.

Raptis et al. (2021) developed GamePass to help people create secure passwords for online applications and tested it against a non-gamified version (OriPass); each version featured low, medium and high levels of image complexity for password creation. GamePass supported login and secure password creation performance and was also a more engaging experience than OriPass. The researchers concluded that gamification in this instance increased people's motivation to perform a mundane task, and that their enjoyment of GamePass supported learning how to select stronger passwords and recall them when logging in again.

With respect to task topic, Chen et al. (2021) explored user engagement with cancer-related messages on Weibo over a 7-week period. Posts were classified by topic (treatment, prevention, social support, smoking, skin cancer, women's cancers), and examined with respect to engagement metrics, i.e., number of retweets, comments and likes. Few messages fostered high levels of engagement, but some of the less discussed topics (social support, smoking) were positively associated with engagement. This suggested that the quantity of posts on a given topic was less salient than factors not explored in the study, e.g., message qualities, users' interest.

Grinberg (2018) observed that different types of news content (e.g., financial, tech) elicited different kinds of user behaviors and used this to construct a measure of semantic information gain. Semantic information gain was found to be a good predictor for reading articles, but not for extended reading of longer texts. Aldous et al., (2019, 2023) looked at audience engagement (i.e., views, likes, comments, and external posting) with news shared via social media platforms, predicting and confirming that user engagement models for one platform may not be transferable to another. The authors showed that some news topics engendered consistently high or low audience engagement across platforms, while others were mixed across platforms (some high, some low). Another study from the online news domain drew upon 5 million reading sessions from 65 news providers in the US, UK, Canada and Australia over a one-month period to examine "story-focused reading," which occurs when users read multiple articles about a particular news development or event" (Lehmann et al., 2017, p. 870). Story-focused reading was driven more by user interests than by the popularity of the news story and resulted in more in-depth reading behaviors. All the aforenoted studies underscore the importance of user interest to sustain longer term content engagement (Sinnamon et al., 2021).

Based on the intrinsic connection between interest and user engagement (Jacques, 1996; O'Brien & Toms, 2008), Edwards and Kelly (2016) manipulated tasks in their user study based on interest. Specifically, undergraduates were asked to pre-rank a list of search tasks from the most to the least interesting and then returned to the lab on a different day to complete four search tasks—two each that they had ranked as least and most interesting. Findings showed that the tasks rated more interesting before the study continued to be evaluated as interesting during the experiment; interesting tasks were also perceived to be more engaging, and students spent more time exploring the SERP and web pages for interesting tasks (though this was not statistically significant).

Another aspect of tasks that has seen some investigation with respect to user engagement is task complexity. During information interactions, users attempt to achieve some level of certainty about the information they want to find (outcome), how to go about looking for it (process), and what information requirements they need to fulfil (e.g., desired source, format, currency, etc.) This notion of *a priori* determinability is linked with task complexity (Byström & Järvelin, 1995). Capra et al., (2017, 2018) manipulated task complexity using different versions of tasks on the same topic. Capra et al. (2017) invited participants to compare items (e.g., classical and neoclassical ballet), dimensions or attributes of the topic, or both; there were also unspecified, open-ended task versions. In a later study, Capra et al. (2018) experimented with distinct dimensions: subjective (e.g., difficulty of ballet postures and movements) or objective (e.g., historical origins of ballet) task dimensions. Although the statistical findings were limited, both studies suggested a negative association between the task versions that were more complex and engagement, but topic also played a role. Unspecified tasks were rated as more interesting pre- and post-search, suggesting open-ended tasks might precipitate engagement (Capra et al., 2018). In addition, task topic had a greater effect on engagement than the task version (O'Brien et al., 2020).

The concept of task has also been used to support information system design and evaluation. Park et al. (2020) analyzed buzz data (i.e., data generated by getting people to talk about a product ("Marketing Buzz," 2024)) collected from Google Assistant and Apple Siri over a three-month period, cognitive work analysis was used to understand the kinds of tasks users were performing with voice assistants. These findings were used to create and test a prototype of a context-aware voice assistant. There was greater self-reported engagement with the version of the voice assistant that provided recommended commands compared to the one that had a guide sentence. The authors speculated that the commands helped users learn how to use the prototype based on the perceived usability ratings of the two systems. In a related study, Qiu et al. (2020) investigated engagement with conversational agents based on task type and user interface; there was one traditional web interface and three conversational interfaces that varied according to response speed and hesitation. There were no differences in user engagement based on the interfaces within each of the four task types, but there were effects of input type (multiple choice vs. free text) and image versus text-based tasks. This led the authors to conclude that task complexity may have influenced people's interactions with the different conversational styles.

3.4 Technology

Technologies are used for different purposes and have different features and affordances. Platform features offer possibilities of the kinds of activities people can do, which sustains users' time on the platform and degree of interaction (Fang et al., 2022). Even within specific technology domains, platforms vary widely. The unique affordances of social media platforms (Facebook, Twitter, Instagram), for instance, require different approaches to distributing online news (Aldous et al., 2019; Boukes et al., 2022) and public health information (Sandoval-Almazan & Valle-Cruz, 2021). Other considerations for technology engagement include whether individual user or community experience is of interest (Johnson & Liew, 2020). This section highlights some strategies used in information interaction studies to foster engagement, specifically storytelling, enhancing information interaction and discovery, and encouraging interactivity.

Storytelling

McDowell defines storytelling as both structural, "narratively patterned information," and functional, "the sharing of information through narrative" (McDowell, 2021, p. 1225). Storytelling has been used to engage people in different digital domains, including social media, digital cultural heritage, and online news.

Nelissen et al. (2018) used the structural elements of a digital newspaper (images, title, end of an article) to invite user feedback on their engagement. Small blue dots beside these interface elements allowed news readers to provide a thumbs up or thumbs down. These ratings were used with time-based measures (e.g., time on article, time on page) and implicit content measures (e.g., proportion of article viewed based on scrolling, article swipes, page swipes) to better understand how readers engaged with news stories. Abidin (2020) also looked at structural elements in their study of storytelling engagement on TikTok. Song lyrics were used to tell a story; rhythm and tempo helped "advance the storyline;" audio memes complemented video memes through ambiance or conveying parody; and audio enabled content organization by marking transitions in time or activities.

Similar storytelling mechanisms have been used in digital cultural heritage. Echeverri and Wei (2020) created a physical prototype, Letters to José, containing digitized handwritten and typed letters and organized these into a cohesive, nonlinear narrative with a main storyline threaded throughout. During the editing and scripting phases, the researchers identified areas where embedding interactivity would enhance the experience. A physical prototype was constructed with tangible artefacts, e.g., a cardboard puppet that symbolized a digital avatar, items that activated audio clips. The authors concluded that artifacts should be carefully considered based on the extent to which they enhance story comprehension, generate user interest through materiality (e.g., sounds, vibrations), and influence user agency. The latter emphasis on user control was also recognized by Agosti et al. (2018), who implemented digital storytelling strategies in a digital heritage collection. They developed narratives through user consultations with expert researchers that resulted in "a series of paths through the content" (p. 361), bringing together artefacts contained in diverse areas of the collection and links to external sources to locate further information. Narratives offered guidance and allowed users to deepen their engagement with the collection but were not prescriptive, thereby facilitating user control and choice.

Interactive film and television enable users to make choices about the direction of a story, rather than viewing it in a pre-determined linear manner. Kolhoff and Nack (2019) surveyed 169 viewers of Netflix's *Bandersnatch*. The film can be watched in default mode (30 minutes) or viewers can direct the plot at key junctures, leading to four alternative endings (maximum runtime 90 minutes). Most respondents (~90%) continued watching the film after the first ending, regardless of whether they were satisfied with it, demonstrating curiosity about the alternative endings. There were also positive associations between the novelty of the interactive movie and self-reported attention and interest.

Enhancing Information Interaction through Search Clarification and Information Discovery

Search clarification is the process whereby searchers determine whether they need to seek clarification and how to create a clarifying question when interacting with an information retrieval system, e.g. web search engine, dialogue system, voice assistant (Sekulić et al., 2021). Information retrieval studies have explored how to facilitate this process with various design affordances. Zamani et al. (2020) tested the effectiveness of a clarification pane embedded in the Bing search engine that posed clarification questions to users in response to their queries. They analyzed over 74.6 million clarification pane impressions (i.e., the number of times the clarification pane was shown to users) based on 5.5 million unique queries to understand and model users' interactions with the clarification pane. Engagement with the clarification pane (operationalized as click behavior) was positively correlated with query length, natural language queries, and faceted queries. Another tactic used by Rossel (2020) was to provide clarifying information and increase the transparency of search results. They experimented with two versions of a knowledge-based recommender system, one with and one without explanations for the recommendations. An A/B test of the two versions was conducted with Amazon Mechanical Turk workers. Having explanations for the recommendations led to higher overall self-reported engagement. Google analytics showed differences in time spent on the two versions and bounce rates, which reinforced the findings that the recommender system with expert-sourced explanations was more usable.

Scott (2022) created a toolkit to facilitate ongoing, dynamic consent for participants in the Rare and Undiagnosed Diseases Study (RUDY). The author reflected that the participants expected researchers to keep their data secure and wanted to be told about changes in their data use, but also disengaged due to "consent fatigue" (p. 109). The Dynamic Consent toolkit was constructed based on assumptions about the role of dynamic consent and engagement in research, namely that dynamic consent increases recruitment, retention, participation, feedback, value to participants, and value to researchers. Each assumption was linked to concrete inputs, activities, outputs, outcomes and impacts. According to the author, "[t]he framework was created to encourage researchers to specify their reasons for using Dynamic Consent and identify metrics that would allow them to measure and justify these assumptions" to support reciprocal information sharing and avoid coercion (Scott, 2022, p. 200).

González-Ibáñez et al. (2017) conducted a within-subjects experiment (n = 20) to compare performance and engagement with a traditional (T) and visual (V) search system. The traditional interface was text-based with a vertical list of search results, whereas the visual interface contained visual representations of search results. With respect to user engagement, the visual interface was rated higher in aesthetic appeal than the traditional system, but there were no overall differences in perceived usability or focused attention. However, a deeper examination of data showed differences in focused attention based on the sequence in which participants interacted with the visual interface, which could indicate familiarity effects on user experience. This study points to the value of considering the sequences and actions that occur during the search process rather than isolated individual behaviors (Zhuang et al., 2018).

Information discovery may be further complicated when collections are not systematically linked (Allison, 2016), and when searching takes place across multiple academic databases on mobile and desktop devices (Gomes et al., 2022). Allison (2016) saw increased engagement (i.e., longer session duration, greater likelihood of visitor return, more visits) when library discover tools harvested metadata to provide access to special collections through the library catalogue compared to relying on other sources to point users toward collections. To combat the challenge of distributed searching, Gomes et al. (2022) created Digital Library Explorer (Dilex), a system that enabled searchers to initiate a search on a mobile device and resume it on a desktop system one week later. Engagement was rated significantly higher than a traditional library search system after both the initial and follow up searches because it enabled searchers to view and monitor their search histories in both session and to "pick up where they had left off with the initial search" in the second session (Gomes et al., 2022, p. 390).

Interactivity

Some studies have experimented with embodied interactions. Koebel and Agotai (2020) tested two prototypes to encourage interactions with historical photographs. One used traditional interaction methods (e.g., mouse input) and the other encouraged embodied interactions (e.g., body movements, gestures, room location). The embodied prototype encouraged greater exploration of the photographs, and increased perceptions of stimulation, novelty, immersion, reward and aesthetic appeal, pointing to the potential for virtual and augmented reality technologies to enhance user experience with digital image collections.

Limerick et al.'s (2019) study of engagement examined materiality with digital signage, digital posters that conveyed high or low levels of interactivity through the delivery of haptic or non-haptic sensations on participants' mobile devices. High levels of interactivity and haptic feedback led to increased self-reported user engagement. Participants also expressed greater satisfaction and information gain when they received haptic feedback, irrespective of interactivity levels.

In addition to haptic feedback, engagement with animation, an "intentional, visual change" in the interface (Wu et al., 2020, p. 1) has been undertaken to help developers evaluate animation designs. Participants viewed and rated their level of engagement with mobile animations and five professional user experience designers were interviewed about why the animations may not have engaged users. Their responses were categorized using the four dimensions of the User Engagement Scale (see Measurement Chapter). For example, under the dimension focused attention, experts may have deemed an animation "too fast;" "distracting," or containing "overwhelming information."

Studies with conversational agents have focused on understanding how people interact with these technologies by comparing different versions. Portela and Granell-Canut (2017) explored engagement with two versions (including one Wizard of Oz version) of a chatbot that facilitated one-on-one conversations via a mobile device. Their main finding was that users preferred the Wizard of Oz version based on the intensity of the conversation (e.g., utterances and social cues). On the other hand, Frummet et al.'s (2024) Wizard of Oz study, which placed participants in a simulated cooking scenario, found that more active conversational agents did not always prompt users to interact more with the agent. Rather, users' satisfaction with the Wizard was related to the kind of task they were performing and whether the information offered by the agent was considered "interesting or useful" at the time.

Meng et al. (2021) focused on optimizing engagement with other types of intelligent assistants, such as Alexa, Siri and Google Home. The authors derived different types of engagement: (1) Fulfillment: meaning the current user request was understood and fulfilled by the system; (2) Continuation: the current user request was understood by the system, but more interactions were required to complete the request; (3) Reformulation: the user must revise or repeat their request because the system did not understand it or returned an inaccurate response; and (4) Abandonment: the user ended the conversation or started a brand new request. To test the classification scheme, the authors collected and annotated data from four intelligent assistants consisting of various task types and scenarios. With engagement metrics for intelligent systems defined through this process, the researchers proposed to automate the classification of utterances to support the evaluation of intelligent assistants at scale in future work.

Chapter Summary
This chapter described characteristics of people, information, tasks and technologies connected with user engagement. Figure 3.2 provides an overview of some of the characteristics highlighted in this review.

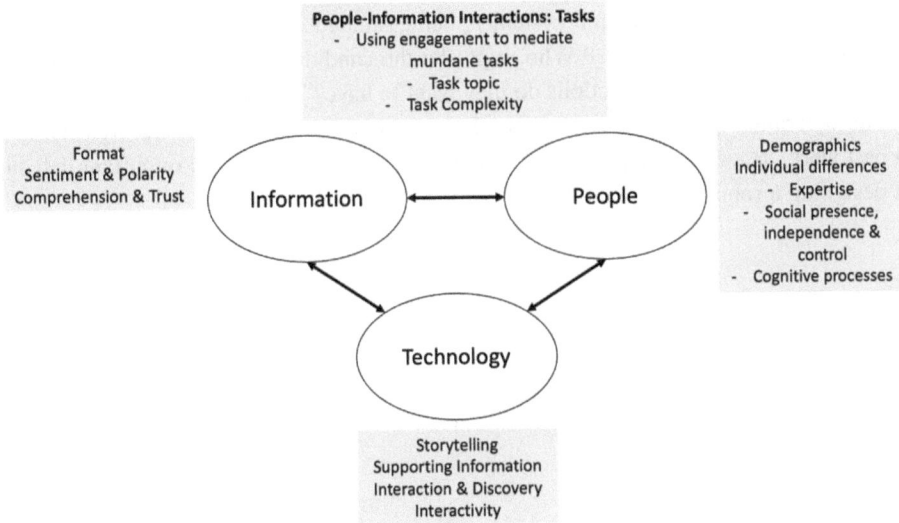

Fig. 3.2. Characteristics of people, information and technology highlighted in this chapter

- Research focusing on *people* has examined how demographics and individual differences affect engagement outcomes or offer a picture of who may or may not be benefiting from/engaging with a system.
- Engagement with *information* may be impacted by the format in which it is presented, the sentiment or polarity expressed in the content, and people's capacity to understand and trust it.
- *Tasks* are activities that propel people to interact with information using information systems. Some research has tried to make mundane tasks more engaging or examined how task topic and complexity affect engagement.
- *Information systems* have used storytelling to encourage engagement, along with strategies to support information interaction through search clarification and discovery, and interactivity.

These characteristics are not a definitive list of the 'key ingredients' of user engagement. Rather, this chapter shows what has been investigated and what insights have been gained through select research studies about user engagement. There are many gaps in the reviewed literature. For instance, users in many of the reviewed studies were crowd-sourced workers or university students, meaning we are limited in our understanding of engagement with other populations. Qualities of people, information and technology are essential for user engagement, but care must be taken in the mixing. For example, employing storytelling or interactivity may or may not be effective depending on the user or information context, nor appropriate for the type of application of interest.

A take-away from this chapter is that readers should consider what unique qualities of people, information and technology are central to their own examination of user engagement. What kind of information system is being studied, and what unique features and affordances does it offer users? Who might be the candidate users of the system? What kinds of information or interactions do they want to have? The answers to these questions should determine the researchers' focus. Being able to situate current research inquiries in past work, as well as the people-information-technology triad, is an important first step in designing a robust research study.

References

Abidin, C. (2020). Mapping Internet celebrity on TikTok: Exploring attention economies and visibility labours. *Cultural Science Journal, 12*(1), 77–103. https://doi.org/10.5334/csci.140

Agosti, M., Orio, N., & Ponchia, C. (2018). Promoting user engagement with digital cultural heritage collections. *International Journal on Digital Libraries, 19*(4), 353–366. https://doi.org/10.1007/s00799-018-0245-y

Aldous, K. K., An, J., & Jansen, B. J. (2023). What really matters?: Characterising and predicting user engagement of news postings using multiple platforms, sentiments and topics. *Behaviour and Information Technology, 42*(5), 545–568. https://doi.org/10.1080/0144929X.2022.2030798

Aldous, K. K., An, J., & Jansen, B. J. (2019). Predicting audience engagement across social media platforms in the news domain. In I. Weber, K. M. Darwish, C. Wagner, E. Zagheni, L. Nelson, S. Aref, & F. Flöck (Eds.), *Social informatics* (Vol. 11864, pp. 173–187). Springer International Publishing. https://doi.org/10.1007/978-3-030-34971-4_12

Allison, D. (2016). OAI-PMH harvested collections and user engagement. *Journal of Web Librarianship, 10*(1), 14–27. https://doi.org/10.1080/19322909.2015.1128867

Amit-Danhi, E. R., & Shifman, L. (2022). Off the charts: User engagement enhancers in election infographics. *Information, Communication and Society, 25*(1), 55–73. https://doi.org/10.1080/1369118X.2020.1761858

Arguello, J., & Choi, B. (2019). The effects of working memory, perceptual speed, and inhibition in aggregated search. *ACM Transactions on Information Systems, 37*(3), 1–34. https://doi.org/10.1145/3322128

Bailey, E. (2017). *Measuring online search expertise* [Doctoral Dissertation]. The University of North Carolina at Chapel Hill.

Begany, G. M., Martin, E. G., & Yuan, X. (Jenny). (2021). Open government data portals: Predictors of site engagement among early users of health data NY. *Government Information Quarterly, 38*(4), 101614. https://doi.org/10.1016/j.giq.2021.101614

Begany, G. M., & Gil-Garcia, J. R. (2021). Understanding the actual use of open data: Levels of engagement and how they are related. *Telematics and Informatics, 63*, 101673. https://doi.org/10.1016/j.tele.2021.101673

Bil-Jaruzelska, A., & Monzer, C. (2022). All about feelings? Emotional appeals as drivers of user engagement with Facebook posts. *Politics and Governance, 10*(1), 172–184. https://doi.org/10.17645/pag.v10i1.4758

Boukes, M., Chu, X., Noon, M. F. A., Liu, R., Araujo, T., & Kroon, A. C. (2022). Comparing user-content interactivity and audience diversity across news and satire: Differences in online engagement between satire, regular news and partisan news. *Journal of Information Technology and Politics, 19*(1), 98–117. https://doi.org/10.1080/19331681.2021.1927928

Byström, K., & Hansen, P. (2005). Conceptual framework for tasks in information studies. *Journal of the American Society for Information Science and Technology, 56*(10), 1050–1061. https://doi.org/10.1002/asi.20197

Byström, K., & Järvelin, K. (1995). Task complexity affects information seeking and use. *Information Processing and Management, 31*(2), 191–213. https://doi.org/10.1016/0306-4573(95)80035-R

Capra, R., & Arguello, J. (2023). *How does AI chat change search behaviors?* (arXiv:2307.03826). arXiv. http://arxiv.org/abs/2307.03826

Capra, R., Arguello, J., & Zhang, Y. (2017). The effects of search task determinability on search behavior. In J. M. Jose, C. Hauff, I. S. Altıngovde, D. Song, D. Albakour, S. Watt, & J. Tait (Eds.), *Advances in information retrieval* (Vol. 10193, pp. 108–121). Springer International Publishing. https://doi.org/10.1007/978-3-319-56608-5_9

Capra, R., Arguello, J., O'Brien, H., Li, Y., & Choi, B. (2018). The effects of manipulating task determinability on search behaviors and outcomes. *The 41st International ACM SIGIR Conference on Research & Development in Information Retrieval* (pp. 445–454). https://doi.org/10.1145/320 9978.3210047

Case, D. O., & Given, L. M. (2016). *Looking for information: A survey of research on information seeking, needs, and behavior* (4th edn). Emerald.

Chen, L., Wang, P., Ma, X., & Wang, X. (2021). Cancer communication and user engagement on chinese social media: Content analysis and topic modeling study. *Journal of Medical Internet Research, 23*(11), e26310. https://doi.org/10.2196/26310

Comello, M. L. G., Qian, X., Deal, A. M., Ribisl, K. M., Linnan, L. A., & Tate, D. F. (2016). Impact of game-inspired infographics on user engagement and information processing in an eHealth program. *Journal of Medical Internet Research, 18*(9), e237. https://doi.org/10.2196/jmir.5976

Dvir, N., Friedman, E., Commuri, S., Yang, F., & Romano, J. (2023). *A predictive model of digital information engagement: Forecasting user engagement with English words by incorporating cognitive biases, computational linguistics and natural language processing.* https://doi.org/10.48550/arXiv.2307.14500

Echeverri, D., & Wei, H. (2020). Letters to José: A design case for building tangible interactive narratives. In A.-G. Bosser, D. E. Millard, & C. Hargood (Eds.), *Interactive storytelling* (pp. 15–29). Springer International Publishing. https://doi.org/10.1007/978-3-030-62516-0_2

Edelson, L., Nguyen, M.-K., Goldstein, I., Goga, O., McCoy, D., & Lauinger, T. (2021). Understanding engagement with U.S. (mis)information news sources on Facebook. *Proceedings of the 21st ACM Internet Measurement Conference* (pp. 444–463). https://doi.org/10.1145/3487552.348 7859

Edwards, A., & Kelly, D. (2016). How does interest in a work task impact search behavior and engagement? *Proceedings of the 2016 ACM on Conference on Human Information Interaction and Retrieval* (pp. 249–252). https://doi.org/10.1145/2854946.2855000

Fang, Z., Costas, R., & Wouters, P. (2022). User engagement with scholarly tweets of scientific papers: A large-scale and cross-disciplinary analysis. *Scientometrics, 127*(8), 4523–4546. https://doi.org/10.1007/s11192-022-04468-6

Frummet, A., Speggiorin, A., Elsweiler, D., Leuski, A., & Dalton, J. (2024). Cooking with conversation: Enhancing user engagement and learning with a knowledge-enhancing assistant. *ACM Transactions on Information Systems, 42*(5), 1–29. https://doi.org/10.1145/3649500

Ghafourian, Y., Hanbury, A., & Knoth, P. (2023). Readability measures as predictors of understandability and engagement in searching to learn. In O. Alonso, H. Cousijn, G. Silvello, M. Marrero, C. Teixeira Lopes, & S. Marchesin (Eds.), *Linking theory and practice of digital libraries* (Vol. 14241, pp. 173–181). Springer Nature Switzerland. https://doi.org/10.1007/978-3-031-43849-3_15

Gomes, S., Boon, M., & Hoeber, O. (2022). A study of cross-session cross-device search within an academic digital library. *Proceedings of the 45th International ACM SIGIR Conference on Research and Development in Information Retrieval* (pp. 384–394). https://doi.org/10.1145/347 7495.3531929

González-IbáñTez, R., Proaño-Ríos, V., Fuenzalida, G., & Martinez-Ramirez, G. (2017). Effects of a visual representation of search engine results on performance, user experience and effort. *Proceedings of the Association for Information Science and Technology, 54*(1), 128–138.

Grinberg, N. (2018). Identifying modes of user engagement with online news and their relationship to information gain in text. *Proceedings of the 2018 World Wide Web Conference on World Wide Web—WWW '18* (pp. 1745–1754). https://doi.org/10.1145/3178876.3186180

Haider, F., Salim, F. A., Luz, S., Conlan, O., & Campbell, N. (2015). High level visual and paralinguistic features extraction and their correlation with user engagement. *2015 IEEE International Symposium on Signal Processing and Information Technology (ISSPIT)* (pp. 326–331).https://doi.org/10.1109/ISSPIT.2015.7394353

Harari, G., & Gosling, S. (2023). Understanding behaviours in context using mobile sensing. *Nature Reviews Psychology, 2*. https://doi.org/10.1038/s44159-023-00235-3

Jacques, R. D. (1996). *The nature of engagement and its role in hypermedia evaluation and design* [Doctoral Dissertation]. South Bank University.

Johnson, E., & Liew, C. L. (2020). Engagement-oriented design: A study of New Zealand public cultural heritage institutions crowdsourcing platforms. *Online Information Review, 44*(4), 887–912. https://doi.org/10.1108/OIR-10-2019-0329

Koebel, K., & Agotai, D. (2020). Embodied interaction for the exploration of image collections in mixed reality (MR) for museums and other exhibition spaces. In C. Stephanidis & M. Antona (Eds.), *HCI International 2020—Posters* (pp. 291–299). Springer International Publishing. https://doi.org/10.1007/978-3-030-50732-9_39

Kolhoff, L., & Nack, F. (2019). How relevant is your choice? In R. E. Cardona-Rivera, A. Sullivan, & R. M. Young (Eds.), *Interactive storytelling* (pp. 73–85). Springer International Publishing. https://doi.org/10.1007/978-3-030-33894-7_9

Lehmann, J., Castillo, C., Lalmas, M., & Baeza-Yates, R. (2017). Story-focused reading in online news and its potential for user engagement. *Journal of the Association for Information Science and Technology, 68*(4), 869–883. https://doi.org/10.1002/asi.23707

Li, Y., & Belkin, N. J. (2008). A faceted approach to conceptualizing tasks in information seeking—Rutgers University. *Information Processing and Management, 44*(6), 1822–1837.

Li, J., Zhang, Y., & Mou, J. (2023). Understanding information disclosures and privacy sensitivity on short-form video platforms: An empirical investigation. *Journal of Retailing and Consumer Services, 72*, 103292. https://doi.org/10.1016/j.jretconser.2023.103292

Limerick, H., Hayden, R., Beattie, D., Georgiou, O., & Müller, J. (2019). User engagement for mid-air haptic interactions with digital signage. *Proceedings of the 8th ACM International Symposium on Pervasive Displays*, 1–7. https://doi.org/10.1145/3321335.3324944

Marchionini, G. (2008). Human–information interaction research and development. *Library and Information Science Research, 30*(3), 165–174. https://doi.org/10.1016/j.lisr.2008.07.001

Marketing buzz. (2024). In *Wikipedia*. https://en.wikipedia.org/w/index.php?title=Marketing_buzz&oldid=1213473637

McCreadie, M., & Rice, R. E. (1999). Trends in analyzing access to information. Part I: Cross-disciplinary conceptualizations of access. *Information Processing and Management, 35*(1), 45–76. https://doi.org/10.1016/S0306-4573(98)00037-5

McDowell, K. (2021). Storytelling wisdom: Story, information, and DIKW. *Journal of the Association for Information Science and Technology, 72*(10), 1223–1233. https://doi.org/10.1002/asi.24466

Meng, R., Yue, Z., & Glass, A. (2021). *Predicting user engagement status for online evaluation of intelligent assistants* (arXiv:2010.00656). arXiv. http://arxiv.org/abs/2010.00656

Nelissen, K., Snoeck, M., Broucke, S. V., & Baesens, B. (2018). Swipe and tell: Using implicit feed-back to predict user engagement on tablets. *ACM Transactions on Information Systems, 36*(4), 1–36. https://doi.org/10.1145/3185153

O'Brien, H. L., & Toms, E. G. (2008). What is user engagement? A conceptual framework for defining user engagement with technology. *Journal of the American Society for Information Science and Technology, 59*(6), 938–955. https://doi.org/10.1002/asi.20801

O'Brien, H. L., Arguello, J., & Capra, R. (2020). An empirical study of interest, task complexity, and search behaviour on user engagement. *Information Processing and Management, 57*(3), 102226.

O'Brien, H. L., Roll, I., Kampen, A., & Davoudi, N. (2022). Rethinking (Dis)engagement in human-computer interaction. *Computers in Human Behavior, 128*, 107109. https://doi.org/10.1016/j.chb.2021.107109

O'Brien, H. L., & McKay, J. (2018). *Modeling antecedents of user engagement* (pp. 73–88). Wiley & Sons, Inc.

Paivio, A. (1991). Dual coding theory: Retrospect and current status. *Canadian Journal of Psychology / Revue Canadienne De Psychologie, 45*(3), 255–287. https://doi.org/10.1037/h0084295

Park, D., Park, H., & Song, S. (2020). A method for increasing user engagement with voice assistant system. In A. Marcus & E. Rosenzweig (Eds.), *Design, user experience, and usability. Design for contemporary interactive environments* (pp. 146–157). Springer International Publishing.

Perski, O., Blandford, A., West, R., & Michie, S. (2017). Conceptualising engagement with digital behaviour change interventions: A systematic review using principles from critical interpretive synthesis. *Translational Behavioral Medicine, 7*(2), 254–267. https://doi.org/10.1007/s13142-016-0453-1

Portela, M., & Granell-Canut, C. (2017). A new friend in our smartphone? Observing interactions with Chatbots in the search of emotional engagement. *Proceedings of the XVIII International Conference on Human Computer Interaction.* https://doi.org/10.1145/3123818.3123826

Qiu, S., Gadiraju, U., & Bozzon, A. (2020). Improving worker engagement through conversational microtask crowdsourcing. *Proceedings of the 2020 CHI Conference on Human Factors in Computing Systems* (pp. 1–12). https://doi.org/10.1145/3313831.3376403

Raptis, G. E., Katsini, C., Cen, A. J., Arachchilage, N. A. G., & Nacke, L. E. (2021). Better, funner, stronger: A gameful approach to nudge people into making less predictable graphical password choices. *Proceedings of the 2021 CHI Conference on Human Factors in Computing Systems.* https://doi.org/10.1145/3411764.3445658

Ritterband, L. M., Thorndike, F. P., Cox, D. J., Kovatchev, B. P., & Gonder-Frederick, L. A. (2009). A behavior change model for internet interventions. *Annals of Behavioral Medicine: A Publication of the Society of Behavioral Medicine, 38*(1), 18–27. https://doi.org/10.1007/s12160-009-9133-4

Robbemond, V., Inel, O., & Gadiraju, U. (2022). Understanding the role of explanation modality in AI-assisted decision-making. *Proceedings of the 30th ACM Conference on User Modeling, Adaptation and Personalization* (pp. 223–233). https://doi.org/10.1145/3503252.3531311

Rossel, F. (2020). *The influence of explanations in recommender systems on user engagement.* [Bachelor Thesis]. Jönköping University. https://urn.kb.se/resolve?urn=urn:nbn:se:hj:diva-50373

Rzepka, C., Berger, B., & Hess, T. (2019). Voice assistant versus Chatbot–examining the fit between conversational agents' interaction modalities and information search tasks. *Information Systems Frontiers, 24*(3), 839–856.

Salehabadi, N., Groggel, A., Singhal, M., Roy, S. S., & Nilizadeh, S. (2022). *User engagement and the toxicity of tweets* (arXiv:2211.03856). arXiv. http://arxiv.org/abs/2211.03856

Sandoval-Almazan, R., & Valle-Cruz, D. (2021). Social media use in government health agencies: The COVID-19 impact. *Information Polity, 26*(4), 459–475. https://doi.org/10.3233/IP-210326

Schellewald, A. (2021). Communicative forms on TikTok: Perspectives from digital ethnography. *International Journal of Communication, 15*(0, 1437–1457.

Scott, A. S. (2022). *Dynamic consent: A mechanism for engagement* [PhD Thesis]. University of Oxford.

Sekulić, I., Aliannejadi, M., & Crestani, F. (2021). *User engagement prediction for clarification in search* (arXiv:2102.04163). arXiv. http://arxiv.org/abs/2102.04163

Short, C. E., Rebar, A. L., Plotnikoff, R. C., & Vandelanotte, C. (2015). Designing engaging online behaviour change interventions: A proposed model of user engagement. *European Health Psychologist, 17*(1), Article 1.

Sinnamon, L., Tamim, L., Dodson, S., & O'Brien, H. L. (2021). Rethinking interest in studies of interactive information retrieval. *Proceedings of the 2021 Conference on Human Information Interaction and Retrieval* (pp. 39–49). https://doi.org/10.1145/3406522.3446031

Sundar, S. S., Bellur, S., Oh, J., Xu, Q., & Jia, H. (2014). User Experience of on-screen interaction techniques: An experimental investigation of clicking, sliding, zooming, hovering, dragging, and flipping. *Human-Computer Interaction, 29*(2), 109–152. https://doi.org/10.1080/07370024.2013.789347

Taki, S., Lymer, S., Russell, C. G., Campbell, K., Laws, R., Ong, K.-L., Elliott, R., & Denney-Wilson, E. (2017). Assessing user engagement of an mHealth intervention: Development and implementation of the growing healthy app engagement index. *JMIR mHealth and uHealth, 5*(6), e89–e89.

Talja, S., Keso, H., & Pietiläinen, T. (1999). The production of 'context' in information seeking research: A met theoretical view. *Information Processing and Management, 35*(6), 751–763. https://doi.org/10.1016/S0306-4573(99)00024-2

Toms, E. G., DuFour, C, Bartlett, J., Fruend, L., & Szigeti, S. (2004). Identifying the significant contextual factors of search. *ACM SIGIR 2004 Workshop on Information Retrieval in Context* (pp. 26–29).

Toms, E. G. (2019). Information activities and tasks. In K. Byström, J. Heinström, & I. Ruthven (Eds.), *Information at work: Information management in the workplace*. Facet Publishing.

Vail, A. K., Grafsgaard, J. F., Wiggins, J. B., Lester, J. C., & Boyer, K. E. (2014). Predicting learning and engagement in tutorial dialogue: A personality-based model. *Proceedings of the 16th International Conference on Multimodal Interaction* (pp. 255–262). https://doi.org/10.1145/2663204.2663276

Vakkari, P. (2003). Task-based information searching. *Annual Review of Information Science and Technology, 37*(1), 413–464. https://doi.org/10.1002/aris.1440370110

Violot, C., Elmas, T., Bilogrevic, I., & Humbert, M. (2024). Shorts versus regular videos on YouTube: A comparative analysis of user engagement and content creation trends. *ACM Web Science Conference*, 213–223. https://doi.org/10.1145/3614419.3644023

Wang, W., Baker, S., & Irlitti, A. (2020). Exploring the effects of user control on social engagement in virtual reality. *32nd Australian Conference on Human-Computer Interaction* (pp. 253–262). https://doi.org/10.1145/3441000.3441076

Wildemuth, B. M. (2004). The effects of domain knowledge on search tactic formulation. *Journal of the American Society for Information Science and Technology, 55*(3), 246–258. https://doi.org/10.1002/asi.10367

Wildemuth, B., Freund, L., & Toms, E. G. (2014). Untangling search task complexity and difficulty in the context of interactive information retrieval studies. *Journal of Documentation, 70*(6), 1118–1140.

Wildemuth, B. M., Kelly, D., Boettcher, E., Moore, E., & Dimitrova, G. (2018). Examining the impact of domain and cognitive complexity on query formulation and reformulation. *Information Processing and Management, 54*(3), 433–450. https://doi.org/10.1016/j.ipm.2018.01.009

Wu, Z., Jiang, Y., Liu, Y., & Ma, X. (2020). Predicting and diagnosing user engagement with mobile UI animation via a data-driven approach. In *Proceedings of the 2020 CHI Conference on Human*

Factors in Computing Systems (pp. 1–13). Association for Computing Machinery. https://doi.org/10.1145/3313831.3376324

Zamani, H., Mitra, B., Chen, E., Lueck, G., Diaz, F., Bennett, P. N., Craswell, N., & Dumais, S. T. (2020). Analyzing and learning from user interactions for search clarification. *Proceedings of the 43rd International ACM SIGIR Conference on Research and Development in Information Retrieval* (pp. 1181–1190). https://doi.org/10.1145/3397271.3401160

Zhuang, M., Toms, E. G., & Demartini, G. (2018). Can user behaviour sequences reflect perceived novelty? *Proceedings of the 27th ACM International Conference on Information and Knowledge Management* (pp. 1507–1510). https://doi.org/10.1145/3269206.3269243

Influences on User Engagement

In the 2012 book, *Addiction by Design: Machine Gambling in Las Vegas,* anthropologist Natasha Dow Schüll contrasts the stories of people whose lives have been affected by gambling technologies with the rhetoric of the machine gambling industry. The book is particularly compelling for thinking about user engagement as it has come to be defined under platform capitalism (Srnicek, 2017).

In "Interior Design for Interior States: Architecture, Ambience, and Affect," Schüll describes the intent behind casinos' maze-like floorplans and aesthetic choices:

> Instead of turning attention away from machines, every aspect of the environment should work to turn attention toward machines, and keep it focused there. From ceiling height to carpet pattern, lighting intensity to aisle width, acoustics to temperature regulation—all such elements [...] should be engineered to facilitate the interior state of the machine zone. (Schüll, 2012, p. 40)

Building on this chapter, "Engineering Experience: The Productive Economy of Player-Centric Design" is a lesson in the mechanics of gambling machines. Specifically, Schüll elaborates three key operations: accelerating play ("keeping the pace" (p. 54)), extending its duration (and preventing disengagement), and increasing the amount of time spent by players (and therefore the amount of money lost by players) by reducing friction around placing bets. These operations work together "to keep patrons playing, and to keep the zone state going" (p. 52). The zone state Dow Schüll speaks of is reminiscent of Flow, but without user agency.

Today 'the zone' and these operations are not only part of gambling spaces and technologies but are embedded in everyday tools and devices. Consider binge watching a

H. O'Brien, *User Engagement Research and Practice*, Synthesis Lectures on Information Concepts, Retrieval, and Services, https://doi.org/10.1007/978-3-031-80916-3_4

Netflix series ("Binge-Watching," 2024) or doomscrolling news on social media ("Doom-scrolling," 2024). The affordances of these platforms allow us to "keep the pace" and spend more time viewing or reading than we had perhaps intended to. Online shopping sites that "helpfully" store our credit card information make future purchases seamless, eliminating "friction" or the need to pause and reflect on potential purchases.

The use of aesthetic and sensory design principles to evoke emotion, capture attention, and foster engagement is not new (Sutcliffe, 2010); nor is the goal of creating a fluid user experience—this has long guided usability research and practice (Norman, 1988; Quesenbery, 2003). But the narrowing of engagement to a behavioral metric has taken place alongside increasingly sophisticated algorithmic and recommender systems that maximize dwell time and clicks (Zhao et al., 2020). Today's digital systems draw from reams of data to personalize, gamify, and tailor the user experience, blurring the boundaries between information and entertainment, fact and fiction, information and advertising.

This chapter discusses elements of the dynamic media landscape, specifically persuasive technologies and gamification, that are essentially redefining user engagement[1]. The goal of this chapter is to move beyond the user-information-technology triad to consider broader influences that are shaping engagement.

(Not Jane Austen's) Persuasion

"Persuasion is as old as humanity"

(Williams, 2021)

The scholarship on persuasion stretches far back in human history but has taken on new life in today's media landscape. Questions around how persuasion works, how people counter persuasive tactics, and how computers have become part of persuasive communication have been investigated across many disciplines, including marketing, health, and human-computer interaction (e.g., Fogg, 1998; Friestad & Wright, 1994; Williams, 2021). My objective is not to provide an in-depth historical or contemporary overview of this topic, but to highlight salient aspects of persuasive technologies in the digital ecosystem that are part of the story of user engagement. Persuasion strategies are used to increase engagement, defined as the sustained and active participation with technologies.[2]

---

[1] Whether this is engagement or problematic use is worthy of further consideration. I would argue that user engagement without agency moves away from the original, conceptually driven essence of what engagement is and toward problematic use.

[2] It is important to acknowledge that persuasion (much like user engagement) is not good or bad but depends on what we do with it (Oinas-Kukkonen & Harjumaa, 2009). Health technologies, for instance, use persuasive tactics to support behavior change and help people achieve health and wellness goals (c.f Aldenaini et al., 2020) and some researchers focus on ethical considerations related to persuasion, including increasing transparency in system design to promote critical literacy (c.f Wang et al., 2023) or enhancing users' awareness and understanding of important issues; for example, Kitkowska et al. (2022) tested different user interface designs to increase users' awareness of

4.1 Persuasive Technologies

Persuasive technologies are "computerized software or information systems designed to reinforce, change or shape attitudes or behaviors or both without using coercion or deception" (Oinas-Kukkonen & Harjumaa, 2009, p. 202). Oinas-Kukkonen and Harjumaa (2009) outline three potential outcomes of persuasive systems:

- They voluntarily reinforce existing behaviors and attitudes,
- They change a person's position on an issue, and
- They shape or create a new attitude or behavior that did not previously exist.

While most of this chapter will focus on the kinds of design strategies used to bring about these outcomes, it is also important to situate the persuasion context that shapes these three outcomes (Oinas-Kukkonen & Harjumaa, 2009).

The Persuasion Context

The *persuasion context* consists of the **Intent**, **Event**, and **Strategy** (Oinas-Kukkonen & Harjumaa, 2009).

- *Intent* refers to the source of the persuasion and type of change desired (e.g., attitude, behavior). Persuasive technologies intentionally persuade, and this intent originates endogenously (from the technology developer), exogenously (from another person), or autogenously (from the self) (Fogg, 1998). Take, for example, the social media platform, Facebook, and influences on current users to continue their engagement (Vanman et al., 2018). From an endogenous perspective, the platform might show us novel information and we might fear missing out on this new content; endogenously, having all our family and friends on Facebook might deter us from leaving for fear of being left out of community news, events, and photo sharing; finally, we might reason that we need a social media presence through Facebook and we don't want to lose the time we have invested building and curating our profile (autogenous).
- The *Event* consists of the user, the use or purpose for engaging, and the technology, each of which brings their own contexts into the interaction (see Chap. 3 for the discussion of how user, information and technology qualities come to bear on an engagement).
- The *Strategy* pertains to the message and how it is being delivered. The message contains information that must be attended to and understood by recipients. Even when a message is received, it may fail to change a person's attitude or behavior. Cinelli et al. (2021), for example, highlighted differences in social media platforms that encourage information spreading versus echo chambers, or "environments in which the opinion,

---

information contained in Terms and Conditions (T&Cs). This is all to say that strategies to encourage both persuasion and transparency can be used to further both user and corporate/industry interests.

political leaning, or belief of users about a topic gets reinforced due to repeated inter-actions with peers or sources having similar tendencies and attitudes" (Cinelli et al., 2021, p. 1), Messages can come through direct and indirect routes, be unobtrusive and incremental, and appeal to reason or emotion. Advertising is a good example of these various message qualities. Much research is dedicated to increasing ad engagement, i.e., click through rates (Chen et al., 2020), and, due to the embeddedness of advertis-ing, e.g., product promotion by social media influencers, it can be difficult to discern ads from information.

Persuasive Design

Persuasive design consists of what Fogg (2002) called the Functional Triad: *tools* that enable us to do new things or make existing activities easier to perform; *media* that conveys sensory (e.g., virtual reality) and symbolic (e.g., text, images) content; and *social actors*, computers that embody human-like qualities and fulfill social roles (e.g., coach, tutor, assistant), follow social rules (e.g., turn taking), or take on animate qualities (e.g., emotions). Computers as social actors persuade by providing positive feedback and social support to a user or modeling a desired attitude or behavior change (Fogg, 2002).

Oinas-Kukkonen and Harjumas (2009) provide further design considerations that enforce the Functional Triad: *Credibility*, *Dialogue*, and guiding users' *Primary Task*.

Credibility

Persuasion knowledge is "personal knowledge about the tactics used in these persuasion attempts" (Friestad & Wright, 1994, p. 1). In essence, persuasion knowledge is our ability to recognize when persuasion is being used and how we want to respond to it. *Credibil-ity* is achieved through the conveyance of "trustworthiness, expertise, surface credibility, real-world feel, authority, third-party endorsements, and verifiability" (Oinas-Kukkonen & Harjumaa, 2009, p. 493).

People often use cognitive heuristics to assess the credibility of content, including its source and media, based on visual, interaction, and navigation cues, e.g., functional hyperlinks, references to reputable sources, the credentials of the author or organization (Hilligoss & Rieh, 2008; Sundar, 2008; Wathen & Burkell, 2002). But the use of AI to "clone" people's voices or likenesses (e.g., David, 2024; Dudha, 2024) and the subtlety of branding in social media ads (Xiao et al., 2024) are examples of why it is increasingly difficult to apply persuasion knowledge.

Dialogue

Dialogue consists of praise, rewards, reminders of the target behavior, recommendations, and relevance (Oinas-Kukkonen & Harjumaa, 2009). An example of this are smartwatches (e.g., Fitbit, Apple watch) that provide us with daily feedback on steps taken, distance covered, hours slept, and stress levels. My Garamond watch reminds me to "Take a break," and encourages me ("Way to go!") when I start to become more active. Social media sites beckon us to return with notifications of new content to view, others viewing our profiles, or new connection requests. Dialogue must provide people with useful, timely information but not overwhelm them with interruptions or unnecessary content. This is reinforced by news stories and YouTube videos providing "self-help" for managing/turning off smartphone and social media notifications that have become burdensome and annoying (Biersdorfer, 2020; Rogers, 2023).

Guiding the Primary Task

Many systems are designed to engage by employing one or more of the following strategies to guide primary tasks with digital systems:

- Reducing complex tasks into more simply tasks to help people more easily achieve a targeted behavior;
- Tunneling, or steering users through an experience or process with "opportunities to persuade along the way" (Oinas-Kukkonen & Harjumas, 2009, p. 492);
- Tailoring information to users' needs and interest;
- Personalizing content and services to users;
- Enabling self-monitoring of goal status and achievement;
- Simulating different scenarios that illustrate cause and effect relationships; and
- Promoting the rehearsal of an attitude or behavior change as practice for an actual, real-world change (Oinas-Kukkonen & Harjumas, 2009).

Tailoring is particularly salient to the discussion about engagement with digital information systems. Tailoring involves:

> creating communications in which information about a given individual is used to determine what specific content he or she will receive, the contexts or frames surrounding the content, by whom it will be presented and even through which channels it will be delivered. (Hawkins et al., 2008, p. 454)

Tailoring aims to make information presented to the user more personally relevant (Hawkins et al., 2008) through *personalization, adaptation* and *recommendation.*

Implicit and explicit data about users (e.g., goals, intentions, preferences) is used to construct user models that shape the content delivered by a system to meet the needs of specific users (i.e., personalization), different users in the same context (i.e., adaptation), or based on what similarly profiled users have viewed, liked, etc. (i.e., recommendation) (Klock et al., 2020). Alternatively, users might have the freedom to select or customize the digital environment according to their needs and preferences (i.e., customization) (Klock et al., 2020; Rodrigues et al., 2021).

Example: Digital Phenotyping

The growing sophistication of algorithmically driven systems means that tailoring is increasingly embedded in digital interactions to induce user engagement, shaping our experience without our conscious awareness. In health research, mobile sensing, digital phenotyping, passive data collection or "just-in-time adaptive interventions" (JITAI) describes the collection and interpretation of mobile sensor data to deliver responsive digital health services (Baumeister & Montag, 2019; Cardoso et al., 2024; Nahum-Shani et al., 2018; Torous et al., 2020).

JITAIs have four main components: (1) decision points, or times in which intervention decisions are made; (2) intervention options, which include the variety of actions or treatment options that can be pursued at any given decision point; (3) tailoring variables, information about users gathered through active (e.g., self-reports), passive, or hybrid data collection methods that determine if and when the system should intervene; and (4) decision rules, the linking of intervention options and tailoring variables to implement adaptations for users (Nahum-Shani et al., 2018, pp. 451–452).

Digital phenotyping may be promising for anticipating user needs in areas such as mental health support: Nahum-Shani et al.'s (2018) argue that personal and contextual vulnerabilities can arise quickly and unexpectedly and may not be recognizable to users themselves. However, it is not enough to collect and interpret behavioral and contextual data; people must be provided with feedback and education to improve health outcomes (Trifan et al., 2019). Nahum-Shani et al.'s (2018) also stated that "many JITAIs have been developed with little empirical evidence, theory, or accepted treatment guidelines" (p. 448), though this limitation may be improving over time. This example points out what is possible through tailoring technologies and why JITAIs might be beneficial in some settings, but also raise ethical and privacy implications about the collection and use of personal data.

4.2   Unifying the Persuasion Context and Persuasive Design: The Case of Mis/Disinformation on Social Media

Disinformation refers to "deliberately generated misleading content disseminated for selfish or malicious purposes" while misinformation is inaccurate content without the intention to spread false information (Sinclair, 2023; Spiro & Starbird, 2023). Rumors are "unverified stories that spread from person to person through informal channels," (Spiro & Starbird, 2023, p. 117).

Spiro and Starbird's (2023) "rumor threat framework" illustrates the "persuasion context," the information, event, system and contextual conditions that perpetuate the spread of rumors.

- Information and event conditions include diminished trust in authoritative or "official" sources (e.g., government) and uncertainty due to lack of concrete evidence around what is happening.
- Contextual features consist of the significance or impact of the rumor on the lives of those involved; familiarity or repetition of the message; new information about events; emotional valence of the rumor; compellingness of the message, often fueled by first-person accounts; and the participatory potential of being able to contribute experiences and interpretations; and
- System effects, specifically the social network position of those sharing the information, and the contributions of algorithmic or network manipulation.

Many tactics are used to spread disinformation: "hahaganda," where comedy, memes and speeches are used to "make light of serious matters, attack others, minimize violence or dehumanize, and deflect blame;" rumor-milling, which involves claiming the communicator has "secret" information that is being "purposefully concealed" from others; and the use of rhetoric to convince others to share it (e.g., "Make this go viral"). Anecdotes and made-up stories also work to draw readers' sympathies and compensate for lack of concrete evidence (Sinclair, 2023).

The persuasion context around and tactics used to promote dis/misinformation and rumors may result in the circulation of both credible and discreditable information. With "few checks and balances in place," information can spread in unpredictable ways and eventually be removed from the "original author and original context" (Zhou et al., 2023, pp. 25–26). Regardless of accuracy, it is all highly engaging.

Ciancone Chama et al. (2019), who showed participants neutral and prejudiced versions of a news video about public transit, found that video engagement was unaffected by biased content and personal stances toward transit. This caused the authors to question whether participants were aware of the bias or at what point they might question the credibility of news. In addition, engagement with content that is familiar or aligned with one's experience perpetuates issues with recommender systems that present people with homogenous content, giving the impression that everyone shares the same views (Ciancone Chama et al., 2019, p. 358). In an era of filter bubbles, polarization, and the "compulsory sociality" of the Internet (Kuntsman & Miyake, 2022, p. 67), we risk taking shortcuts that perpetuate mis/disinformation. Hassoun et al. (2023) found that information overload made GenZers seek information "in quickly absorbable forms" that were "emotionally manageable" and "personally relevant" (p. 6). They "crowdsourced their credibility judgments by observing how others reacted to the same information" (p. 8). Their findings raised concerns that young adults are more susceptible to mis/disinformation if it is more important to fit in than to cultivate and apply persuasion knowledge.

Overall, mis/disinformation on social media illustrates how the persuasion context and persuasive technologies come together, and how human and technological actors in the system create, spread, react to and engage with mis/disinformation to perpetuate is continuance.

4.3   Gamification

Gamification is employed in digital technologies, from digital health applications (Fleming et al., 2017; Schmidt-Kraepelin et al., 2019) to dating apps (Garda & Karhulahti, 2021), to increase engagement. Hamari (2019) defines gamification broadly as "an intentional process of transforming any activity, system, service, product, or organizational structure into one which affords positive experiences, skills, and practices similar to those afforded by games, and is often referred to as the gameful experience" (p. 1). Games provide players with goals and feedback through rules, rewards like badges and points, and challenges or quests, and are designed with narrative and visually aesthetic elements and around different kinds of social interactions (e.g., collaborating or competing with other players, role playing) (Deterding et al., 2011; Hamari, 2019; Schwarz et al., 2020).

Game mechanics, design and aesthetics are used in non-game settings to motivate people to do a task (Medlar & Głowacka, 2021), change a behavior (Schwarz et al., 2020), or encourage learning (Chapman et al., 2023; Goslen et al., 2023; Hallifax, 2020). Spryidonis and Daylamani (2021), for example, drew upon serious games to encourage designers to engage with web accessibility guidelines (WCAG 2.0).

"In a nutshell, gameful approaches are used to enhance more functional activities or experiences, thereby making them more engaging and more desirable" (Macey et al., 2024, p. 2). The relationship between engagement and gamification has been explored in different contexts, showing which aspects of games appear to encourage or deter engagement. Xiao et al. (2022) summarized findings from human-computer interaction research according to four main areas:

- Features such as role playing, avatars, story, and personified objects and content used to create immersive, interactive worlds that promote attitude or behavior changes;
- Rewards in the form of badges, levels, and social reputation, that motivate and incentivize system use;
- The use of gamification to induce a flow state to prolong use; and
- Features that involve goal setting and balance player skills and challenge to support users' self-efficacy and performance.

A systematic review by Schwarz et al. (2020) concluded that features that encouraged engagement with serious games to promote health were different for youth and adults. In general, however, higher levels of engagement were associated with narrative, challenge and reward game mechanics, resonance with characters, and use of multimedia.

Using gamification to engage users is not without its drawbacks. Schwarz et al. (2020) cautioned that health information featured in games must be non-judgmental and focus on positive outcomes of health behaviors (rather than unhealthy behaviors), while Hallifax (2020) stated that games that fail to consider users' preferences and expectations may demotivate or disengage users in learning environments.

Gamification can also be used in ways that negatively affect end users, primarily by encouraging problematic use. Reviglio and Agosti (2020) drew upon research linking the design affordances of online games and social media to compulsion loops. In such loops, dopamine pathways in the brain are activated by features of the application that deliver unpredictable rewards; for instance, sensational or negative emotional content, or features that encourage vying for popularity through likes and upvoting or compel social participation and content sharing. Related to the workings of gamification is the concept of *gamblification*:

> the (increased) presence of gambling (or gambling-related content) in non-gambling contexts in order to realise desired outcomes. It incorporates two main aspects: affective (employing cultural values/signifiers of gambling); and effective, (employing gambling games and activities). (Macey & Hamari, 2024)

While both gamification and gambilification employ game-like design strategies, gamblification emphasizes external motivation through the promise of real-word rewards, which can result in personal and financial loss (Macey et al., 2024). The introduction of gamblification into the (non-gambling) digital ecosystem brings us full circle with the introduction of this chapter and the operations identified by Schüll (2012), reinforcing the assertion that they are present beyond casino and gambling environments.

4.4   Dancing with Algorithms: The Case of TikTok

All sociotechnical systems are shaped by people, and people are shaped by technologies. In today's dynamic digital landscape where systems are designed to engage through persuasion, tailoring, gamification, and personalization, there are many effects on users. Some of these effects may seem like old arguments. Reams of research papers have been written on the negative effects of television on children's attention spans and social behaviors. These arguments are revisited with each new media but there are also key differences. Social media has invited new conceptions of the "user," demonstrating both active and passive engagement, and both kinds of engagement make platforms like TikTok particularly "affectively sticky" or engaging (Kendall, 2021, p. 44).

Users as active agents

Web 2.0 gave people the opportunity to be both content creators and recipients. Today's "influencers" represent the new "conduits of knowledge" (Abidin, 2020, p. 78). The ability to engage in content creation has disrupted traditional models of information dissemination and notions of expertise, and algorithmic possibilities have changed the ways in which creators interact with distribution channels.

Abidin (2020) conducted a digital ethnology of TikTok influencers' labor, observing four kinds of practices: ownership, algorithmic, interactive, and legacy. Ownership practices involved "stak[ing] their authorship and attribution claims, or desires for acknowledgement and credit, when others borrow, reuse, adapt from, or remix a piece of content that they originated," e.g., "please credit" (Abidin, 2020, p. 86). Algorithmic practices attempt to "persuade and trigger the platform's algorithm to work in their favor" (Abidin, 2020, p. 88), e.g., posting at certain times of day, adding non-salient hashtags to videos to encourage videos to "trend" (Klug et al., 2021). Interactive practices include other people, or what Abidin refers to as "chart jacking" "wherein TikTokers encourage others to engage with specific posts to get them to 'climb' the ranks on a stream, to overshadow posts that they want to suppress, or to negotiate the 'mainstream' use of a specific audio meme or filter" (Abidin, 2020, p. 81). Finally, legacy practices consisted of importing microcelebrity and influencer actions from other Internet spaces into TikTok to build a brand. These practices are used as ways to cultivate the presentation of self and to get and stay noticed, i.e., to maximize engagement (Klug et al., 2021).

Active engagement is not limited to influencers or content creators. Bhandari and Bimo (2022) showed that TikTok users spent time following creators, liking content, or trying to get on a particular "side" of TikTok.

Passive Engagement

"Get ready with me while I do my morning routine"

In a 45-second video, TikTok influencer @saraglamour123[3] records her daily routine as she prepares to head to work. Viewers watch as Sara gets out of the shower, applies her makeup, and prepares her breakfast, all while the video is overlaid with her voice describing her routine and all the products she uses. By not speaking or looking directly at the camera, Sara creates an environment where her viewers feel like they are privy to the intimate and relatively mundane routine of getting ready alongside a friend.

Content such as the above vignette exemplifies how TikTok influencers and content creators engage their audiences through monotonous everyday life tasks. Looking at the popularity of TikTok during the Covid-19 pandemic, Kendall (2021) describes how such uneventful videos helped alleviate "the bored body problem" of lockdown by organizing people's attention and framing the collective experience of sheltering in place (p. 42).

---

[3] Fictional, not a real TikTok content creator.

Montag et al. (2021) argue that the design affordances of the platform (e.g., "Likes," personalized content on the "For Me" page, and the sheer volume of content) contribute to immersive and prolonged user experiences. Users feel a sense of community and belonging through the platform even when they are not actively sharing or commenting on videos or following other people. This led Kang and Lou (2022) to conclude that "User engagement should also entail passive or non-quantifiable indicators like browsing, interests (or lack of interests) in certain contexts and skipping behaviors" (p. 9). By this statement, one can only presume that the authors are referring not to engagement but to its measurement and finding ways to assess experience beyond behavioral markers.

In the same way that the TikTok algorithm is central to active users, it is also crucial in more passive user experiences. Bhandari and Bimo (2022) described the increasing humanizing of the algorithm over time by participants in their study, which created both positive and negative responses in users. Sometimes the algorithm felt too restrictive, repetitive, or unable to deliver content to meet their needs (Bhandari & Bimo, 2022), while at other times algorithms were welcomed to reduce the cognitive load of filtering and evaluating content (Hassoun et al., 2023). Another study by Zhao and Wagner (2022) showed that, over time, TikTok users assigned greater agency to the algorithm to determine what content they viewed. This reliance on the algorithm presents a decoupling of context from use (Bhandari & Bimo, 2022), signally a kind of user engagement that is less agentic and reflective. This will undoubtedly prompt new questions about the role of TikTok in information provision and use.

Chapter Summary

This chapter looked at the broader technological context in which engagement research is unfolding. Moving beyond the people-technology-information triad, I discussed elements of persuasive technologies and gamification, and used TikTok as an example of how active and passive forms of engagement are playing out in algorithmically mediated environments.

Information is framed in ways that can influence our actions and is delivered using technologies that employ a range of design strategies to personalize, customize, and adapt content to us—as defined by the data we supply to online platforms. Sometimes this tailoring is welcomed and helpful, and at other times it can be disruptive and even creepy (Woźniak et al., 2021). And the line between these states is blurry:

> The research recognizes the problem of how difficult it might be to draw a boundary between a nudge and a dark pattern, and some of the methods used by UI [user interface] designers, such as undeceiving coercion, are sometimes not even recognized as dark patterns (Kitkowska et al., 2022, p. 17).

The question of whether smartphones and social media is "addictive" is an ongoing debate in research studies (e.g., Bhargava & Velasquez, 2021; Busch & McCarthy, 2021; Hansen,

2022; Montag et al., 2024) and the popular press.[4] It is unknown where these discussions should or will take us as a society regarding technology regulation. But it brings us back to the notion of how engagement has been redefined as a signal and an economic driver rather than an experience. Returning to Schüll's (2012) work that led this chapter, it invites reflection on the power of design to engage, how we use that power, and who benefits in the end from engaging design.

References

Abidin, C. (2020). Mapping internet celebrity on TikTok: Exploring attention economies and visibility labours. *Cultural Science Journal, 12*(1), 77–103. https://doi.org/10.5334/csci.140

Aldenaini, N., Alqahtani, F., Orji, R., & Sampalli, S. (2020). Trends in persuasive technologies for physical activity and sedentary behavior: A systematic review. *Frontiers in Artificial Intelligence, 3.* https://doi.org/10.3389/frai.2020.00007

Baumeister, H., & Montag, C. (2019). *Digital phenotyping and mobile sensing—New developments in psychoinformatics.* Springer.https://doi.org/10.1007/978-3-030-31620-4

Bhandari, A., & Bimo, S. (2022). Why's everyone on TikTok now? The algorithmized self and the future of self-making on social media. *Social Media and Society, 8*(1), 205630512210862–205630512210862. https://doi.org/10.1177/20563051221086241

Bhargava, V. R., & Velasquez, M. (2021). Ethics of the attention economy: The problem of social media addiction. *Business Ethics Quarterly, 31*(3), 321–359. https://doi.org/10.1017/beq.2020.32

Biersdorfer, J. D. (2020, February 5). How to take control of your notifications. *The New York Times.* https://www.nytimes.com/2020/02/05/technology/personaltech/control-phone-notifications.html

Binge-watching. (2024). In *Wikipedia.* https://en.wikipedia.org/w/index.php?title=Binge-watching&oldid=1229879637

Busch, P. A., & McCarthy, S. (2021). Antecedents and consequences of problematic smartphone use: A systematic literature review of an emerging research area. *Computers in Human Behavior, 114,* 106414. https://doi.org/10.1016/j.chb.2020.106414

Cardoso, T. de A., Kochhar, S., Torous, J., & Morton, E. (2024). Digital tools to facilitate the detection and treatment of bipolar disorder: Key developments and future directions. *JMIR Mental Health, 11*(1), e58631. https://doi.org/10.2196/58631

Chapman, J. R., Kohler, T. B., Rich, P. J., & Trego, A. (2023). Maybe we've got it wrong. An experimental evaluation of self-determination and Flow Theory in gamification. *Journal of Research on Technology in Education,* 1–20. https://doi.org/10.1080/15391523.2023.2242981

Chen, X., Mitra, S., & Swaminathan, V. (2020). Metadata matters in user engagement prediction. *Proceedings of the 43rd International ACM SIGIR Conference on Research and Development in Information Retrieval* (pp. 1529–1532). https://doi.org/10.1145/3397271.3401201

Ciancone Chama, A. G., Monaro, M., Piccoli, E., Gamberini, L., & Spagnolli, A. (2019). Engaging the audience with biased news: An exploratory study on prejudice and engagement. In H.

---

[4] Over the past few months, school boards in the Canadian province of Ontario are suing social media companies for endangering young people's mental well-being. In the United States, New York State just passed laws regulating social media's algorithms and use of data supplied by young users (Gollom, 2024; Paul, 2024).

Oinas-Kukkonen, K. T. Win, E. Karapanos, P. Karppinen, & E. Kyza (Eds.), *Persuasive technology: Development of persuasive and behavior change support systems* (pp. 350–361). Springer International Publishing. https://doi.org/10.1007/978-3-030-17287-9_28

Cinelli, M., De Francisci Morales, G., Galeazzi, A., Quattrociocchi, W., & Starnini, M. (2021). The echo chamber effect on social media. *Proceedings of the National Academy of Sciences, 118*(9), e2023301118. https://doi.org/10.1073/pnas.2023301118

David, E. (2024, May 22). *Lawyers say OpenAI could be in real trouble with Scarlett Johansson.* The Verge. https://www.theverge.com/2024/5/22/24162429/scarlett-johansson-openai-legal-right-to-publicity-likeness-midler-lawyers

Deterding, S., Dixon, D., Khaled, R., & Nacke, L. (2011). From game design elements to gamefulness: Defining "gamification." *Proceedings of the 15th International Academic MindTrek Conference: Envisioning Future Media Environments* (pp. 9–15). https://doi.org/10.1145/218 1037.2181040

Doomscrolling. (2024). In *Wikipedia*. https://en.wikipedia.org/w/index.php?title=Doomscrolling& oldid=1231175089

Dudha, A. (2024, June 8). Sask. Urging federal government to ban AI voice cloning ahead of elections. *CBC News.* https://www.cbc.ca/news/canada/saskatoon/sask-urging-federal-government-to-ban-ai-voice-cloning-ahead-of-elections-1.7228835

Fleming, T. M., Bavin, L., Stasiak, K., Hermansson-Webb, E., Merry, S. N., Cheek, C., Lucassen, M., Lau, H. M., Pollmuller, B., & Hetrick, S. (2017). Serious games and gamification for mental health: Current status and promising directions. *Frontiers in Psychiatry, 7*, 215. https://doi.org/10.3389/fpsyt.2016.00215

Fogg, B. (1998). Persuasive computers: Perspectives and research directions. *Proceedings of the SIGCHI Conference on Human Factors in Computing Systems* (pp. 225–232). https://doi.org/10.1145/274644.274677

Fogg, B. J. (2002). *Persuasive technology: Using computers to change what we think and do.* Morgan Kaufmann [Imprint].

Friestad, M., & Wright, P. (1994). The persuasion knowledge model: How people cope with persuasion attempts. *Journal of Consumer Research, 21*(1), 1–31. https://doi.org/10.1086/209380

Garda, M. B., & Karhulahti, V.-M. (2021). Let's play tinder! Aesthetics of a dating app. *Games and Culture, 16*(2), 248–261. https://doi.org/10.1177/1555412019891328

Gollom, M. (2024, April 7). Ont. School boards are trying to knock down the social media giants. Do their cases stand a chance? *CBC News.* https://www.cbc.ca/news/canada/school-boards-suing-soc ial-media-1.7164151

Goslen, A., Henderson, N., Rowe, J., Zhang, J., Hutt, S., Ocumpaugh, J., Wiebe, E., Boyer, K. E., Mott, B., & Lester, J. (2023). Enhancing engagement modeling in game-based learning environments with student-agent discourse analysis. In N. Wang, G. Rebolledo-Mendez, V. Dimitrova, N. Matsuda, & O. C. Santos (Eds.), *Artificial intelligence in education. Posters and Late Breaking Results, Workshops and Tutorials, Industry and Innovation Tracks, Practitioners, Doctoral Consortium and Blue Sky* (pp. 681–687). Springer Nature. https://doi.org/10.1007/978-3-031-36336-8_105

Hallifax, S. (2020). *Adaptive gamification of digital learning environments.* [Doctoral Dissertation]. Université Jean Moulin Lyon 3.

Hamari, J. (2019). Gamification. In *The blackwell encyclopedia of sociology* (pp. 1–3). Wiley. https://doi.org/10.1002/9781405165518.wbeos1321

Hansen, K. (2022, December). *Our social media addiction.* Harvard Business Review. https://hbr.org/2022/11/our-social-media-addiction

Hassoun, A., Beacock, I., Consolvo, S., Goldberg, B., Kelley, P. G., & Russell, D. M. (2023). Practicing information sensibility: How gen Z engages with online information. *Proceedings of the*

2023 CHI Conference on Human Factors in Computing Systems (pp. 1–17). https://doi.org/10. 1145/3544548.3581328

Hawkins, R. P., Kreuter, M., Resnicow, K., Fishbein, M., & Dijkstra, A. (2008). Understanding tailoring in communicating about health. *Health Education Research, 23*(3), 454–466. https://doi. org/10.1093/her/cyn004

Hilligoss, B., & Rieh, S. Y. (2008). Developing a unifying framework of credibility assessment: Construct, heuristics, and interaction in context. *Information Processing and Management, 44*(4), 1467–1484. https://doi.org/10.1016/j.ipm.2007.10.001

Kang, H., & Lou, C. (2022). AI agency versus human agency: Understanding human–AI interactions on TikTok and their implications for user engagement. *Journal of Computer-Mediated Communication, 27*(5), zmac014. https://doi.org/10.1093/jcmc/zmac014

Kendall, T. (2021). From binge-watching to binge-scrolling. *Film Quarterly, 75*(1), 41–46. https:// doi.org/10.1525/fq.2021.75.1.41

Kitkowska, A., Högberg, J., & Wästlund, E. (2022). Online terms and conditions: Improving user engagement, awareness, and satisfaction through UI design. *CHI Conference on Human Factors in Computing Systems* (pp. 1–22). https://doi.org/10.1145/3491102.3517720

Klock, A. C. T., Gasparini, I., Pimenta, M. S., & Hamari, J. (2020). Tailored gamification: A review of literature. *International Journal of Human-Computer Studies, 144*, 102495. https://doi.org/10. 1016/j.ijhcs.2020.102495

Klug, D., Qin, Y., Evans, M. C., & Kaufman, G. (2021). Trick and please. A mixed-method study on user assumptions about the TikTok algorithm. *Web Science Conference* (pp. 84–92). https:// doi.org/10.1145/3447535.3462512

Kuntsman, A., & Miyake, E. (2022). *Paradoxes of digital disengagement: In search of the opt-out button.* University of Westminster Press. https://doi.org/10.16997/book61

Macey, J., Adam, M., Hamari, J., & Benlian, A. (2024). Examining the commonalities and differences between Gamblification and gamification: A theoretical perspective. *International Journal of Human–Computer Interaction*, 1–14. https://doi.org/10.1080/10447318.2024.2346690

Macey, J., & Hamari, J. (2024). Gamblification: A definition. *New Media and Society, 26*(4), 2046–2065. https://doi.org/10.1177/14614448221083903

Medlar, A., & Głowacka, D. (2021). Game over?: A review of gamification in information retrieval. *ACM SIGIR Forum, 55*(2), 1–18. https://doi.org/10.1145/3527546.3527551

Montag, C., Yang, H., & Elhai, J. D. (2021). On the psychology of TikTok use: A first glimpse from empirical findings. *Frontiers in Public Health, 9.* https://www.frontiersin.org/articles/10.3389/ fpubh.2021.641673

Montag, C., Demetrovics, Z., Elhai, J. D., Grant, D., Koning, I., Rumpf, H.-J., M. Spada, M., Throuvala, M., & van den Eijnden, R. (2024). Problematic social media use in childhood and adolescence. *Addictive Behaviors, 153*, 107980. https://doi.org/10.1016/j.addbeh.2024.107980

Nahum-Shani, I., Smith, S. N., Spring, B. J., Collins, L. M., Witkiewitz, K., Tewari, A., & Murphy, S. A. (2018). Just-in-time adaptive interventions (JITAIs) in mobile health: Key components and design principles for ongoing health behavior support. *Annals of Behavioral Medicine, 52*(6), 446–462. https://doi.org/10.1007/s12160-016-9830-8

Norman, D. A. (1988). *The psychology of everyday things.* Basic Books.

Oinas-Kukkonen, H., & Harjumaa, M. (2009). Persuasive systems design: Key issues, process model, and system features. *Communications of the Association for Information Systems, 24*(1). https://doi.org/10.17705/1CAIS.02428

Paul, K. (2024, June 20). New York signs parental control of 'addictive' social media feeds into law. *The Guardian.* https://www.theguardian.com/us-news/article/2024/jun/20/new-york-social-media-bill

Quesenbery, W. (2003). The five dimensions of usability. In M. Albers & B. Mazur (Eds.), *Content and complexity* (pp. 81–102). Routledge.

Reviglio, U., & Agosti, C. (2020). Thinking outside the black-box: The case for "Algorithmic Sovereignty" in social media. *Social Media + Society, 6*(2), 205630512091561. https://doi.org/10.1177/2056305120915613

Rodrigues, L., Palomino, P. T., Toda, A. M., Klock, A. C. T., Oliveira, W., Avila-Santos, A. P., Gasparini, I., & Isotani, S. (2021). Personalization improves gamification: Evidence from a mixed-methods study. *Proceedings of the ACM on Human-Computer Interaction, 5*(CHI PLAY), 1–25. https://doi.org/10.1145/3474714

Rogers, K. (2023, September 26). *Teens are exhausted by phone notifications but don't know how to quit, report finds.* CNN. https://www.cnn.com/2023/09/26/health/teen-hundreds-of-phone-notifications-report-wellness/index.html

Schmidt-Kraepelin, M., Thiebes, S., & Sunyaev, A. (2019). Investigating the relationship between user ratings and gamification—A review of mHealth apps in the apple app store and google play store. *Proceedings of the 52nd Hawaii International Conference on System Sciences.*

Schüll, N. D. (2012). *Addiction by design: Machine gambling in Las Vegas.* Princeton University Press. https://www.jstor.org/stable/j.ctt12f4d0

Schwarz, A. F., Huertas-Delgado, F. J., Cardon, G., & DeSmet, A. (2020). Design features associated with user engagement in digital games for healthy lifestyle promotion in youth: A systematic review of qualitative and quantitative studies. *Games for Health Journal, 9*(3), 150–163. https://doi.org/10.1089/g4h.2019.0058

Sinclair, H. C. (2023, December 7). Disinformation is rampant on social media—A socialpsychologist explains the tactics used against you. *The Conversation.* https://theconversation.com/disinformation-is-rampant-on-social-media-a-social-psychologist-explains-the-tactics-used-against-you-216598

Spiro, E., & Starbird, K. (2023, May 11). Rumors have rules. *Issues in Science and Technology.* https://issues.org/rumors-research-misinformation-spiro-starbird/

Spyridonis, F., & Daylamani-Zad, D. (2021). A serious game to improve engagement with web accessibility guidelines. *Behaviour and Information Technology, 40*(6), 578–596. https://doi.org/10.1080/0144929X.2019.1711453

Srnicek, N. (2017). The challenges of platform capitalism: Understanding the logic of a new business model. *Juncture, 23*(4), 254–257. https://www.ippr.org/articles/the-challenges-of-platform-capitalism

Sundar, S. S. (2008). Self as source: Agency and customization in interactive media. In *Mediated interpersonal communication* (Vol. 9780203926864, pp. 58–74). Routledge Taylor & Francis Group. https://doi.org/10.4324/9780203926864

Sutcliffe, A. (2010). *Designing for user engagement: Aesthetic and attractive user interfaces.* https://doi.org/10.1007/978-3-031-02188-6

Torous, J., Michalak, E. E., & O'Brien, H. L. (2020). Digital health and engagement—Looking behind the measures and methods. *JAMA Network Open, 3*(7), e2010918–e2010918. https://doi.org/10.1001/jamanetworkopen.2020.10918

Trifan, A., Oliveira, M., & Oliveira, J. L. (2019). Passive sensing of health outcomes through smartphones: Systematic review of current solutions and possible limitations. *JMIR mHealth and uHealth, 7*(8), e12649. https://doi.org/10.2196/12649

Vanman, E. J., Baker, R., & Tobin, S. J. (2018). The burden of online friends: The effects of giving up Facebook on stress and well-being. *The Journal of Social Psychology, 158*(4), 496–507. https://doi.org/10.1080/00224545.2018.1453467

Wang, H., Miao, P., Jia, H., & Lai, K. (2023). The dark side of upward social comparison for social media users: An investigation of fear of missing out and digital hoarding behavior. *Social Media + Society, 9*(1), 20563051221150420. https://doi.org/10.1177/20563051221150420

Wathen, C. N., & Burkell, J. (2002). Believe it or not: Factors influencing credibility on the Web. *Journal of the American Society for Information Science and Technology, 53*(2), 134–144. https://doi.org/10.1002/asi.10016

Williams, J. (2021). Ethical dimensions of persuasive technology. In C. Véliz (Ed.), *Oxford handbook of digital ethics.* https://doi.org/10.1093/oxfordhb/9780198857815.013.15

Woźniak, P. W., Karolus, J., Lang, F., Eckerth, C., Schöning, J., Rogers, Y., & Niess, J. (2021). Creepy technology: what is it and how do you measure it? *Proceedings of the 2021 CHI Conference on Human Factors in Computing Systems* (pp. 1–13). https://doi.org/10.1145/3411764.3445299

Xiao, R., Wu, Z., & Hamari, J. (2022). Internet-of-gamification: A review of literature on IoT-enabled gamification for user engagement. *International Journal of Human-Computer Interaction, 38*(12), 1113–1137. https://doi.org/10.1080/10447318.2021.1990517

Xiao, S., Wang, J., Wang, J., Chen, R., & Chen, G. (2024). On the consensus of synchronous temporal and spatial views: A novel multimodal deep learning method for social video prediction. *Information Processing and Management, 61*(1), 103534. https://doi.org/10.1016/j.ipm.2023.103534

Zhao, Y., Zhou, Y.-H., Ou, M., Xu, H., & Li, N. (2020). Maximizing cumulative user engagement in sequential recommendation: An online optimization perspective. *Proceedings of the 26th ACM SIGKDD International Conference on Knowledge Discovery and Data Mining* (pp. 2784–2792). https://doi.org/10.1145/3394486.3403329

Zhao, H., & Wagner, C. (2022). How TikTok leads users to flow experience: Investigating the effects of technology affordances with user experience level and video length as moderators. *Internet Research, 33*(2), 820–849. https://doi.org/10.1108/INTR-08-2021-0595

Zhou, K., Wilson, T., Starbird, K., & Spiro, E. S. (2023). Spotlight Tweets: A lens for exploring attention dynamics within online sensemaking during crisis events. *ACM Transactions on Social Computing, 6*(1–2), 1–33. https://doi.org/10.1145/3577213

Approaches to Measuring User Engagement   5

> *"When a measure becomes a target, it ceases to be a good measure"*
>
> – Goodhart's Law

In *Measuring User Engagement,* Lalmas et al. (2014) characterized three broad approaches to measuring user engagement: self-report methods (e.g., questionnaires, interviews); physiological methods (e.g., eye tracking, recording heart rate, skin conductance, and facial expressions) (Carrino et al., 2017)); and capturing user behavior through interactions with online platforms (e.g., click through, dwell time, logins, and interaction engagement (Tian et al., 2021a, 2021b)). Perugia et al. (2022) categorized these methods into three corresponding approaches based on human response systems: (1) experiential or subjective, (2) peripheral or physiological and (3) behavioral or expressive.

These types of methods are frequently used to measure user engagement. A systematic review of 351 journal and conference papers published in the Association of Computing Machinery (ACM) Digital Library confirmed that self-report methods were the most used (n = 157; 41.3%), followed by behavioral methods (n = 119; 31.3%), and physiological measures (n = 104, 27.3%) (Doherty & Doherty, 2019). Self-report measures are sometimes referred to as "subjective," while data collected about usage and physiology is called "objective" (Yeager & Benight, 2018) but, the terms subjective and objective should not be used to infer measurement quality (Lalmas et al., 2014). All methods are prone to biases, whether due to human or machine error in how data is collected, cleaned and interpreted. Many researchers who use machine learning methods are acknowledging

H. O'Brien, *User Engagement Research and Practice*, Synthesis Lectures on Information Concepts, Retrieval, and Services, https://doi.org/10.1007/978-3-031-80916-3_5

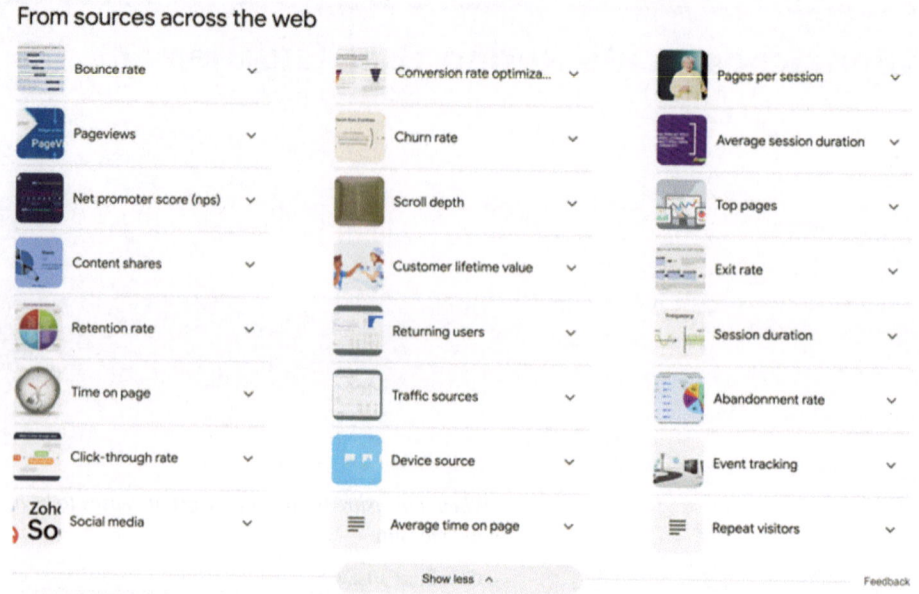

From sources across the web

Bounce rate	Conversion rate optimiza...	Pages per session
Pageviews	Churn rate	Average session duration
Net promoter score (nps)	Scroll depth	Top pages
Content shares	Customer lifetime value	Exit rate
Retention rate	Returning users	Session duration
Time on page	Traffic sources	Abandonment rate
Click-through rate	Device source	Event tracking
Social media	Average time on page	Repeat visitors

Show less ∧   Feedback

Fig. 5.1. Screenshot of Google search for "web user engagement metrics" (August, 8, 2024).

and attempting to mitigate this in AI systems (Mehrabi et al., 2022). No method is perfect, and the researchers' best approach is to be transparent about the methods used and their benefits and drawbacks.

Employing different methods and measures of user engagement in the same study can help mitigate the biases in any one approach. Increasingly, more studies are using mixed methods, and recognizing the value of qualitative approaches in understanding user experience (Doherty & Doherty, 2019; Wei et al., 2020). This is an important finding because engagement has come to be narrowly defined as usage, especially by industry and media. For example, a user experience article identified "the top 20 user engagement metrics that [online businesses and services] should be tracking," including bounce, user retention and conversion rates (see Fig. 5.1); only two metrics listed: customer satisfaction and net promoter score (NPS) involved strategies to gather feedback directly from users (Koç, 2024). This has reduced engagement to a metric rather than a rich multidimensional concept to describe a particular kind of user experience.

In this chapter, I provide an overview of how self-report, behavioral and physiological approaches are currently used to study engagement. This chapter compliments earlier work by Lalmas et al. (2014) on measuring user engagement, but also reflects some advancements in evaluating computer-mediated interaction, such as the increased availability and use of eye tracking, and mobile and web analytic tools that gather usage and physiological data (Gunawardena et al., 2022). The landscape of generative AI and machine learning is evolving rapidly (Shao et al., 2022), and has brought new measurement opportunities. Given the increase in mixed methods, I also examine how and why researchers are combining self-report, behavioral and psychological methods.

5.1 Self-report Methods

Self-report methods ask people to describe their feelings, behaviors or attitudes towards a technology or experience. Common self-reporting methods used in user engagement research include interviews, focus groups, questionnaires, ecological momentary assessments, and think aloud/think after protocols, which are often used as part of experimental or usability studies (Lalmas et al., 2014; Yardley et al., 2016). Readers are invited to consult additional resources to learn about the steps involved in using these methods, but, in brief:

- Interviews/focus groups are structured, semi-structured or unstructured conversations with people or groups (Connaway & Radford, 2021);
- Think aloud/think after protocols involves people verbally expressing their thoughts and feelings while they complete a task (think aloud) or immediately after they complete a task (think after) (Ericsson & Simon, 1980, 1984); and
- Questionnaires feature carefully selected, worded and ordered sets of questions to gather information from a sample of a population" (Connaway & Oxford English Dictionary, 2007; Peterson, 2000; Radford, 2021). Psychometric questionnaires are a special kind of theoretically derived questionnaire that measures a social or psychological phenomena (DeVellis, 2003).[1] Psychometric scales are useful for understanding complex constructs comprised of multiple dimensions or attributes, such as user engagement. There are at least 40 user experience (UX) questionnaires that cover multiple or specific characteristics of experience, including user engagement (Schrepp, 2020),[2] with the User Engagement Scale (UES) being the most widely used (see sidebar).

Self-report methods can result in the collection of quantitative data, like when we use a rating scale in a questionnaire, or we can collect qualitative data, like verbal responses to

---

[1] Psychometric questionnaires must be rigorously developed and evaluated for reliability and validity. Several sources provide an overview of the scale development process, including DeVellis (2003), McCay-Peet et al. (2014), O'Brien & McCay-Peet (2017), and O'Brien & Toms (2010). 7/8/24 5:28:00 PM.

[2] Other self-report questionnaires include the TWente Engagement with Ehealth and Technologies Scale (TWEETS) (Kelders et al., 2020), the Questionnaire for Gender-based Engagement (Alserri et al., 2019), Multidimensional Student Engagement Scale (Astleitner, 2020), and the UX Context Scale (UXCS) (Lallemand & Koenig, 2020).

interview questions. In some cases, we may have both qualitative and quantitative data, e.g., questionnaires and dairies can consist of closed- and open-ended questions.

There are some well-known biases with self-report methods. Respondents may inflate their level of agreement with a survey question, provide what they think is the "right" answer (i.e., social desirability), or be unable to accurately recall a past event (Kelly, 2009). In the case of think aloud/think after protocols, there is the risk that verbalizing one's thoughts and feelings could affect performance on the primary task or change thoughts and feelings. Also, some thoughts can be difficult to verbalize, and it is not a typical process for us to talk aloud as we do something with another person in the room! Despite their limitations, an advantage of self-report measures is that they consider users' perceptions, feelings and attitudes about an event, experience, or technology.

Example: The User Engagement Scale (UES)

The User Engagement Scale (UES) is one of the most enduring and widely adopted questionnaires for measuring user engagement. It was developed as part of my doctoral research and based on an in-depth literature review, an exploratory interview study, and two large-scale survey studies with users of digital technologies (O'Brien, 2008; O'Brien & Toms, 2010), and evaluated using prescribed statistical methods (DeVellis, 2003). The original UES consisted of 31 items and purported to measure six dimensions of engagement: aesthetic appeal, focused attention, novelty, perceived usability, felt involvement, and endurability.

I continued to evaluate the robustness of the UES in online search and news environments (O'Brien & Cairns, 2015; O'Brien & Toms, 2013) and other researchers began using and reporting on their use of the UES (c.f., Landa-Avila & Cruz, 2017; Wiebe et al., 2014). As a result, I (O'Brien, 2016) analyzed the UES' strengths and weaknesses, and then partnered with colleagues Paul Cairns and Mark Hall to improve the UES (O'Brien et al., 2018). We employed contemporary statistical tools to re-analyze data from my PhD studies and a new data set gathered from a three-year digital library project. The revised UES retained the original 31 items but confirmed four rather than 6 dimensions: perceived usability, aesthetics appeal, focused attention, and reward. We proposed a brief version of the questionnaire and provided more information on scoring and interpreting the UES. The UES-Long Form (UES-LF) and Short Form (UES-SF) are contained as an appendix in the open-access journal article describing our critical examination and revision of the UES (O'Brien et al., 2018).

Since its revision, the UES has been used by researchers in several domains (e.g., psychology, health) and continues to be a reliable and valid instrument (Andrade et al., 2019; Klein et al., 2019). It has also been translated into multiple languages, including German (Holdener et al., 2020), French (Fontaine et al., 2020), Italian (Gabrielli et al., 2021) and Portuguese (Miranda et al., 2021), with promising findings related to the psychometric qualities of the translated versions. These works collectively highlight the need to consider linguistic and social-cultural factors when translating and evaluating questionnaires such as the UES. For example, Fontaine et al. (2020) replaced two items in the UES-SF's focused attention dimension with two items from the long version after observing that the literal translations of these SF items into French lacked comprehensibility. Authors leading the translation of the UES into other languages followed established cross-cultural adaptation frameworks that included content and language experts at different stages of the process, and practiced reverse translation strategies (i.e., translating the English version into the target language, and then back into English).

5.2 Why Use Self-report Measures to Study User Engagement?

Interviews, questionnaires, and think aloud/think after protocols are employed to study user engagement for the same reasons that we use these methods in other studies: to ask people how they think and feel about an experience with a technology, and to gain insights into these aspects experience. Self-report methods can highlight why people engage and under what circumstances and provide the means to triangulate other forms of data. Another important use is to inform design.

Understanding why and how people engage

Researchers have used interviews, alone or in combination with observational data, to gain more insight from users about their experiences. This information can be helpful for appreciating how engagement shifts over time, and how different aspects of technologies and the social context contribute to such shifts.

Martinez-Comeche and Ruthven (2021) conducted a study using in-depth interviews and questionnaires with 30 Spanish citizens to understand their everyday life interactions and long-term engagement with WhatsApp. Day to day, people's propensity to engage with WhatsApp was related to their ability to focus their attention on the app, balancing the importance of WhatsApp conversations with daily demands and distractions. Continued use of WhatsApp depended on the enjoyment that people derived from the app (e.g., entertainment, humor) and characteristics of the technology, i.e., perceived usefulness and ease of use.

In another study, Zhao et al. (2022) found differences in participants' pre- and post-adoption attitudes of immersive technologies. They conducted observations and critical incident interviews with medical students about their interactions with virtual reality (VR), augmented reality (AR), and mixed reality (MR) technologies. They found that participants' initial reasons for engaging with immersive technologies were for entertainment purposes and out of curiosity. However, post-adoption, participants talked about benefits to their learning, i.e., reinforcing practical skills for unfamiliar procedures, bolstering memory through visual representations of medical knowledge, and socialization, including working as part of a team and learning from peers and domain experts.

Finally, Said and Çarçani (2020) combined interviews and observations to propose a two-dimensional framework for engagement in distributed cooperative work that incorporated social and technological interactions. They found that the first dimension, interacting with others, was facilitated by shared communication cues around turn-taking; having a visible structure or agenda for the meeting; and being interested in and able to understand what was happening. The authors identified three technology factors that affected engagement: visibility, i.e., people keeping their camera feeds on; communication between members through speaking but also reading/writing short messages; and trust, which was related to the nature of the multitasking people were engaged in, e.g. writing notes in a Word document about the meeting versus being "mentally absent". The addition of interview data offered a more comprehensive view of how social and technological factors interacted to shape engaging experiences.

Triangulating User Behavior and Self-Report Measures

Multiple studies have used self-report questionnaires and interaction data. For example, the User Engagement Scale (UES) has been employed in studies with interactive media (Carlton et al., 2019, 2021) and information retrieval systems (Arguello & Choi, 2019; Arguello & Crescenzi, 2019; Thomas et al., 2016; Zhuang et al., 2017) to examine the relationship between specific dimensions of engagement (e.g., focused attention, perceived usability) and specific behaviors. The combination of self-report and behavior measures has allowed researchers to understand the relationships between these distinct data sources, triangulate the methods to ensure the robustness of the findings, and build predictive machine learning models.

Zhuang et al. (2016) sought to derive a more parsimonious set of behavior measures and automate data collection in interactive information retrieval settings based on the UES's dimensions (Zhuang, 2016). In their study of the novel search system, "WikiSearch," they created "low" and "high" engagement groups based on median UES scores. Using 37 behaviors related to click behavior, querying, results retrieved, and time, the researchers trained a Random Forest model and calculated the top 10 behavior measures per UES sub-scale. Despite some measures appearing on multiple lists, the authors concluded that "different dimensions of engagement reflect behavior differently" (p. 1964). For example, perceived usability and novelty were best predicted by query related features, while felt involvement was best predicted by dwell time (Zhuang et al., 2017). Arguello and colleagues also mapped associations between UES dimensions and groups of behavioral metrics across multiple studies. Collectively, they observed that searchers seemed to equate self-reported engagement with the behavioral effort required to complete search tasks (Arguello & Crescenzi, 2019; O'Brien et al., 2020a, 2020b), which has implications for designing search systems to support user engagement with complex tasks.

Informing Design

Self-report methods can be especially important in the design process to understand how people currently or wish to engage with technology, and to appreciate how engagement may evolve over time. O'Brien et al. (2024) traced the design evolution of Virtual Online Communities for Aging Life Experience (VOCALE), a digital health intervention. VOCALE incorporates problem-solving therapy and peer support in an online community set up. Four 8-week rounds with participants were carried out: rounds one-three focused on health self-management for older adults, and round four centered on caregiving of people with Lewy Body Dementia. Iterative feedback and behavioral interactions from participants over the course of the four rounds identified "pain points," such as issues with navigation, privacy concerns, perceptions of relevance in the delivery of the problem-solving therapy, and prompted design changes. O'Brien et al. (2024) explored the impact on participants learning and social engagement through post-intervention interviews, highlighting areas for future work but also the value of qualitative, iterative and participatory approaches in designing for engagement.

Self-report methods may be especially crucial in participatory design approaches. Participatory design:

> Includes activities where users, designers, and researchers collaborate toward shared goals. Mutual learning between these groups is hence important as is the emphasis that Participatory Design starts with the current practices of people in groups and organizations and uses future alternatives for joint reflection and action, in critical and inclusive ways. (Bødker et al., 2022)

An example of using community-informed, participatory methods comes from Shiri and Stobbs (2018). They described a partnership, the Digital Library North project, between university researchers and the Inuvialuit Cultural Resource Centre (ICRC). The goal of the project was to provide regional information infrastructure to support the organization and discovery of materials and access for local communities. The partnership developed a digital library in three phases (information gathering, prototyping, community demonstration) that incorporated formal (e.g., usability tests, interviews) and informal (e.g., open house events) evaluation strategies. User engagement was defined according to users' motivations for engaging with the digital library's collections. Users' motivations for engaging with the digital library's collections included: "interactivity," "listening," "looking at pictures," "reading," "sharing information," "sharing media," "storytelling," and "staying connected" (p. 445). These themes were used to examine how the digital interface could promote storytelling and sharing through features that enabled social bookmarking, item downloads and posting comments on items.

5.3   Behavioral Methods

Behavioral methods involve collecting data on user interactions with websites, databases, apps, digital libraries, digital health interventions, and more. These interactions are measured using metrics such as logins, mouse clicks, dwell time, session length, pages visited, scrolling, keystrokes, and the use of specific features, such as the "back button" on a webpage or the publication date filter of a database. In general, studying interactions can demonstrate the breadth of features a user has engaged with, and which features have been accessed more than others. User engagement is typically defined based on the number and frequency of such activities and time spent using a technology (e.g., total time but also time spent on specific features, length of unique sessions, and time between unique sessions) (O'Brien et al., 2020a, 2020b).

In this section, I outline both the potential and drawbacks for behavioral measures. Specifically, I will highlight the ways in which the growing sophistication of statistical methods are enabling deeper understandings of user behavior in combination with other kinds of data and over time. Next, I will touch upon some of the considerations for using behavioral data, focusing on their interpretation.

The Potential of Behavioral Methods

Researchers are moving away from "raw counts of usage" in favor of more nuanced approaches to understanding behavior, including using Machine Learning (ML) and statistical techniques (e.g., cluster analysis) to create user profiles or clusters, model use trajectories or pathways, and perform more temporal analyses (Chen et al., 2019; Ponciano & Brasileiro, 2014; Sanatkar et al., 2019; Tian et al., 2021a, 2021b).

Clustering user data

Behavioral trajectories or clusters can be used to categorize technology users as a first step to understanding the nature of their engagement. Chen et al. (2019) clustered individuals' behaviors based on general use of a digital health intervention, Intelli-Care (Low Usage, High Usage), and engagement with two of its most used apps. The researchers compared the clusters to see if there were differences in mental health outcomes (e.g., depression, anxiety), observing that health benefits may be derived from digital interventions interactions even when behavioral engagement is limited.

Behavioral differences can also be examined when self-report data is used to create clusters. Tian et al., (2021a, 2021b) asked undergraduate students to self-report their level of frustration[3] after interacting with learning modules in a computer science course. This led to four groupings based on frustration level (low vs. high) and dynamism vs. consistency across modules. The clusters were used to explore students' problem solving and help-seeking behaviors and workspace explorations, noting differences in the number of

---

[3] Frustration has been studies in tandem with engagement in learning and search environments (Baker et al., 2010; Edwards, 2015).

programming interactions being performed (low vs. high) and students' frustration levels (up vs. down) over time. High, persistent frustration kept people engaged in help-seeking (rather than workplace exploration) and experiencing high ups and downs in frustration was associated with less activity, potentially a sign of "giving up" or disengaging. These findings have implications for monitoring behaviors in learning management systems to support learners.

Machine Learning Approaches

Researchers are beginning to use machine learning (ML) techniques to identify factors related to the user, system, and user-system interaction to model and test the best set of engagement predictors in specific contexts. Computational models can show how engagement outcomes "vary across individuals and populations, settings, and time;" in other words, "What works, how well, for whom, in what settings, for what behaviors, and why?" (Michie et al., 2017, p. 9).

It should be noted that ML studies view engagement as one of many metrics that contribute to system success and defines it as "an action taken by a user on an item, e.g. click, like, comment, retweet, upvote, downvote, dwell time, watch time" (Cunningham et al., 2024). In this context, engagement is prized for being active, longer (i.e., more time spent by the user), and of higher effort (e.g., posting a longer comment) and intent (i.e., taking an action like bookmarking a page), and may not be associated with quality, which might be operationalized independently from activity as informativeness, toxicity, etc. (Cunningham et al., 2024).

ML techniques have the potential to devise new metrics for engagement. For example, Wu (2021) used ML to devise a novel metric, relative engagement (the rank percentile of a video relative to other videos of the same length based on average watch percentage) for video recommender systems. Using a sample of over 5 million YouTube videos, Wu concluded that relative engagement was stable over time, significantly correlated with measures of video quality and that early watch patterns were indicative of future video engagement. In addition, Milli et al. (2021) questioned the value of different engagement signals (likes versus clicks) in constructing recommender systems. They created a latent variable model that aggregated engagement signals with explicit user feedback on Twitter to consider "value" as the goal of evaluation rather than engagement.

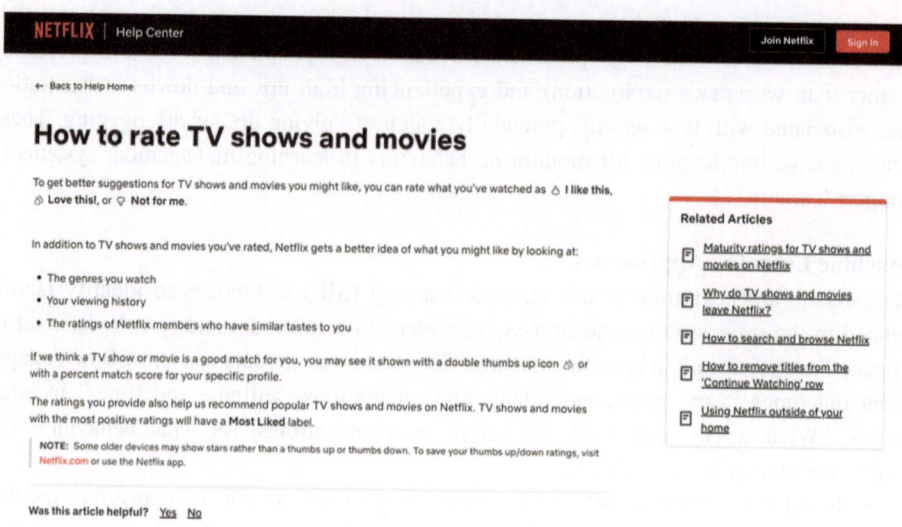

Fig. 5.2 How Netflix personalizes viewer recommendations

Example: The Netflix Recommender System

Back in 2009, a student of mine did a brilliant project for a course I was teaching on information behavior. These were the days long before Spotify, Netflix and other streaming services. The student observed that it can be difficult to specify what you are looking for when it comes to entertainment content, especially when you are "just browsing" and don't have a song, movie or show in mind. He devised a small study that used card sorting to think about how music made people *feel* and explored whether emotional words could be used to support information seeking needs.[4] Today, of course, many streaming services do this. Not only do we search for/are presented with genre selections (e.g., "classic rock," "comedy"), but also with affective descriptors (e.g., "steamy," "thrilling").

Modern-day, algorithmically driven services seem to know us better than we know ourselves. Gomez-Uribe and Hunt (2016) outline algorithms that support Netflix viewer engagement: personalized video ranker (PVR), top-N video ranker, continue watching, trending now, video-video similarity, and page generation of recommended selections. Some of these algorithms help us discover content based on our past selections and what other people have watched and enjoyed, while others help us to re-engage with what we have been viewing but have temporarily disengaged from (Fig. 5.2). Given the popularity of Netflix, these personalization strategies appear to be working (Chong, 2021).

---

[4] Of course, public librarians and proponents of readers' advisory have long known this! See Ross, 1999.

Tracing Behaviors over Time

A common measure of engagement is time spent using an application. Duration on its own has been critiqued because it can have multiple interpretations, such as indicating absorption or disorientation/frustration (Grinberg, 2018; O'Brien & Lebow, 2013). It could also signal a lack of *agentic engagement*, where a user feels like they are not in control of the interaction yet unable to disengage (O'Brien et al., 2022). For instance, Goetzen et al. (2023) compared the perceived and actual time users spent on TikTok. They found that people who were more accurate in their time estimates reported more frequent sessions and fragmented use, and tended to spend less time on the platform than those with less accurate estimates. But more sophisticated measures of time can show how users allocate their resources, how engagement changes over time, and how to adapt systems to changing user needs.

Investigating temporal components of user interaction can shed light on whether users are disengaging quickly, i.e., abandoning features or the application, or re-engaging with an application in future (Pham et al., 2019). Vassio et al. (2021) looked at Italian Influencers on Facebook and Instagram, their posts, user interactions with the posts, and average followers for both platforms. They found that 50% of interactions occurred within a few hours after content creation (4 hrs. for Facebook, 2 hrs. for Instagram), meaning posts no longer attracted attention after 1–2 days. As a result, interactions with posts within the first 15–60 minutes could be used to predict content popularity.

Temporal measures can also shed more light on the engagement process (Tang et al., 2020). Syn (2021) analyzed posts on the Centers for Disease Control and Prevention (CDC) Facebook page and users' reactions (e.g., shares, comments, use of Facebooks' reaction features) amidst the unfolding COVID-19 pandemic from January to June 2020. The 6-month observation period revealed changes in both posts and reactions to posts. Over time, posts became more instructional/promotional and "liking" posts became more common than sharing them.

Time-based approaches can also be used to adapt systems to changing user needs. Hallifax (2020) developed a personalized gamification approach to enhance the mathematics engagement of high school students using the online e-learning platform, LudiMoodle. Hallifax (2020) identified behavioral metrics (e.g., number of quizzes successfully completed, number of quizzes completed on the first try), and categorized them into three engagement factors: wide learning, performance, and deep learning, which were calculated for each learner for each lesson. Learner engagement was compared to engagement with previous lessons and other learners during the same session. If learners were in the lower third of the class, teachers were prompted to consider adaptations for them to re-engage them in learning.

5.4   Drawbacks of Behavioral Measures

Since users tend to perform the same kinds of actions (e.g., clicks, scrolls) across applications and domain areas, researchers must carefully consider the motivations of target users and the system features they expect or would like them to engage with in specific settings. For instance, a researcher designing a health app may focus on the extent to which users track behaviors related to a health condition or goal, such as sleep, diet, exercise, or medication adherence, or whether user notifications encourage tracking behavior. On the other hand, an information retrieval specialist might be more interested in whether adding a new feature to a search system results in deeper engagement with content based on decreased time on the search results page and increased interactions and time spent on content page views.

There are further considerations in the use and interpretation of behavioral data:

- *Differentiating Clicks and Engagement*: While clicks are often seen as proxies of user engagement, "not all clicks are equal" (Zhou et al., 2021, p. 101). In other words, clicks are indicative of some action, but, on their own, do not explain the alignment between users' goals and actions. Number of interactions has been shown to be inversely related with dwell time (Wu, 2021), indicating the importance of using other contextual cues to interpret such measures.
- *Passive Engagement*: Much emphasis is placed on active engagement, but studies have demonstrated how passive engagement has value. Deng et al. (2020) showed how "Lurkers"—users who, based on conventional measures of engagement, were less engaged—are essential to the functioning of Q&A sites. These users read content, follow questions, topics, and other users, and 'favorite' content, all of which are actions that encourage content contributions from others. These passive forms of engagement may be significant at both the individual and community levels in terms of meaningful engagement, but disregarded if engagement is defined solely as activity. Another example comes from Rivera et al. (2022) who used interviews to contextualize Latinx participants' Facebook use patterns in relation to cancer information. Quantitatively, participants were more passive in their use: they were more likely to view than interact with the content (e.g., sharing, liking commenting). But interviews revealed that passive interactions with content were meaningful to participants. They cautioned that basing engagement solely on likes, comments and shares provided "a limited explanation of the impact of health information in the social media landscape" on specific user communities (Rivera et al., 2022, pp. 8–9).
- *Platform Dependent Metrics*: Engagement metrics may be platform-dependent due to the unique affordances of various technologies. Puntha et al. (2021) used some of the same engagement metrics to study Instagram and YouTube (e.g., number of media uploads by content creators), but each platform's design necessitated using some distinct measures and interpreting the same measures in different ways.

Overall, it is crucial to think about the limits of behavioral measures and to foreground users and their contexts:

> Behavioral measures represent one important measure, but do not effectively capture affective and cognitive investment. To understand where people are starting from emotionally and cognitively is particularly important in mental health. In a patient experiencing more severe symptoms, it can be a major accomplishment to simply login into an app and connect with a support person, never mind explore interactive features, such as quizzes, read content, and journal. For some people, this single action itself might be highly influential, especially if the program or app is recovery focused. Other users may benefit from frequent, sustained interactions with the app that allow them to better understand and monitor their wellness needs and triggers. In both of these instances, each user 'gets what they need' from the technology, but their patterns of engagement look very different. (Torous et al., 2020, p. 1)

5.5 Physiological Methods

Physiological measures assess brain activity, heart rate, respiration, electrodermal activity, facial expressions, physical activity, eye movements and pupil dilation. Collectively, these measures may indicate arousal, movement or visual attention and tend to operate automatically and below users' level of consciousness (Yardley et al., 2016). Methods used to collect physiological signals include electroencephalography (EEG) and functional magnetic resonance imaging (fMRi) (brain activity), facial electromyography (fEMG) and video recordings (facial expressions), eye tracking technologies (eye movement, pupil diameter), and wearable sensors. Readers wishing to learn more about these methods and their general applications in information science and human-computer interaction may refer to articles such as Mostafa and Gwizdka (2016), Navarro et al. (2021), Novák et al. (2023), Wu et al. (2019), and Ye et al. (2024).

A barrier to measuring human physiology has been the cost and accessibility of measurement devices. However, eye tracking and brain-computer interface (BCI) tools are becoming increasingly available, less costly, and more feasible to use outside of controlled laboratory environments (Castiblanco Jimenez et al., 2023; Georges et al., 2020).

Mobile sensing has evolved to collect user data unobtrusively, at scale, and over time due to the ubiquity of smartphones, smart home devices (e.g., Alexa), wearables like smartwatches (e.g., Google's Fitbit), and sensors embedded in public spaces.[5] Mobile sensors include onboard sensors (e.g., accelerometer, Bluetooth, Wi-Fi, global positioning system (GPS), camera, microphone, gyroscope, light) and log data (e.g., app use, screen time, battery level, and incoming/outgoing calls and texts) (Dogan et al., 2017; Harari & Gosling, 2023; Trifan et al., 2019). Mobile sensing data and techniques are being used

---

[5] Ramírez-Moreno et al. (2021) provide an overview of the many sensors embedded in urban infrastructures to monitor and manage traffic, energy and resource consumption, security, etc. as part of building "smart cities" or "intelligent cities".

to investigate well-being (e.g., physical activity, smoking cessation), mental health (e.g., depression) and personality traits (Harari & Gosling, 2023; Nahum-Shani et al., 2018).

Mobile sensing has the advantage of being high in ecological validity. Data are collected in naturalistic settings using devices that are part of daily routines; they do not require users to input data, which can make them less burdensome and reduce the potential bias of self-report methods (Harari & Gosling, 2023). At the same time, mobile sensing has drawbacks, particularly with respect to navigating ethical and privacy considerations (Harari & Gosling, 2023; Ksibi et al., 2021), and overcoming challenges related to data management and the technical knowledge required to collect, clean, and interpret sensing data (Harari & Gosling, 2023). It is argued that more work is needed to turn these signals into "meaningful" measures for phenomena of interest, and to ensure the reliability of the machine learning models that "crunch" this data (Harari & Gosling, 2023, p. 774). Some researchers are attempting to amend this limitation by combining mobile sensing data and self-reports. McDaniel et al. (2023) looked at parents' smartphone use (e.g., total hours of phone use, use of video, gaming, or social media applications) in 15-minute intervals with daily surveys of how participants spent their day (e.g.., time at work, with their child, with their spouse, sleeping, etc.). Statistical analysis focused on the integration of the two kinds of data to contextualize phone use in relation to participants' desire to change phone behaviors.

This section looks at how researchers have used physiological measures in the study of user engagement, and how physiological data has been used in concert with other kinds of data to provide a more holistic understanding of physiological signals.

5.6   Physiological Measures and User Engagement

Eye tracking studies have focused specifically on eye movements to distinguish types of content, e.g., boring vs. engaging (Kunze et al., 2015), sensitive vs. non-sensitive (Syn, 2016) and to explore the effects of individual differences on people's capacity to engage with different kinds of information visualizations (Lallé et al., 2017).

Kunze et al. (2015) conducted an experiment using excerpts from three Victorian novels to engender boredom and three contemporary texts to stimulate engagement, combining self-report, eye tracking (i.e., blink activities) and physiology (nose temperature change) measures. Syn (2016) used eye tracking to investigate how Facebook users approached less sensitive (allergies, influenza) and more sensitive health topics (HIV and medicine, chemotherapy for cancer treatment). Both studies used small samples (<10), but did observe some physiological differences. While Kunze et al. (2015) did not find differences in eye blinks between conditions, they associated nose temperature changes with increased workload and lower engagement. Syn (2016) found that fixation counts were higher for the highly sensitive topics than for the less sensitive subjects; the presence of an image within the post also increased users' attention.

While these studies focused on examining user attention and interest in relation to specific types of content, Lallé et al. (2017) used eye tracking to help capture the influence of individual characteristics (i.e., spatial memory, visual working memory, perceptual speed, visualization literacy, and visual scanning ability) on participants' satisfaction and decision making with information visualization tasks. They asked participants (n = 166) to explore and rate three city transit scenarios using different kinds of visualizations, e.g., deviation chart, map. Users with lower spatial memory, visual scanning ability, perceptual speed, visualization literacy, and visual working memory exhibited reduced and less extensive gaze behavior when comparing the map and deviation chart using the experimental MetroQuest interface. In this case, eye tracking was viewed as a way to identify aspects of information visualizations that deterred engagement based on individual differences, and how this knowledge could be used to adapt and support the comprehension and use of information visualizations.

Some researchers have used eye tracking with other physiological measures. For example, De Carolis et al. (2019) examined the facial expressions, head pose and eye gaze of 86 participants watching videos to train a deep learning model of "engaged" and "non-engaged" behavior. Next, computer science students watched one or more videos with different modalities: video-slides (no teacher), video-lesson (technical lecture with teacher) and video-lesson-TED-style (emotional lecture with teacher); self-reported engagement was also captured. The authors found correspondence between perceived engagement and physiological measures. For instance, greater levels of engagement based on facial expressions were related to higher self-reported engagement. There were also differences in engagement between the three video modalities, with the video-slides and technical lecture inducing greater levels of stress for participants than the TED-style video.

Example: Lifelogging

"Lifelogging" describes data collection through cameras and wearable sensors. These multiple data points are analyzed using deep learning approaches and may be shared with users to help them track and manage behavior, monitor quality of life and aid memory (Ksibi et al., 2021). Ksibi et al.'s (2021) overview of lifelogging considers the role of information retrieval systems and digital storytelling in presenting users' data to them: "Digital storytelling targets insights into users through examining their Lifelogs and mining their daily activities and lifestyles" (p. 62637), but this requires information retrieval capabilities to construct relevant, non-redundant, high-quality images to engage the life logger.

We see examples of lifelogging in our daily lives. Google Photos often collates images with similarities based on year ("Best of 2019"), location ("Into the Wild" to collate pictures taken on forest walks), etc. Health technologies are another space where our data is mined and presented back to us. The Oura ring "gives your body a voice" (Oura Ring, n.d) by "continually collecting data on over 20 biometrics that directly impact your wellbeing, day and night" (How Does Oura Ring Work, n.d.). While lifelogging technologies present ways to engage with memories and monitor health, they are certainly not without their detractors, especially where user privacy is concerned (Loeffler, 2021; Zuckerman & McGrady, 2024).

5.7   Making Sense of Physiological Data

Perugia et al. (2022) contend that engagement metrics, including eye gaze, posture, facial expressions, non-verbal communications (e.g., nodding) are typically drawn from healthy participant samples. They investigated people with mild-moderate dementia engaged in activities requiring different social and cognitive skills and featuring different levels of challenge and interactive components. Drawing from human-robot interaction, they identified behaviors like touch and manipulation (e.g., tapping, holding), vocalizations (e.g., humming), emotional expressions (e.g., yelling) and agitating behaviors (handwringing), that could provide a deeper understanding of experience, and were able to show concurrent validity between behavioral observations and physiological data (i.e., electrodermal activity (EDA) and accelerometer signals).

Several other studies have examined the correspondence between physiological and self-report measures with mixed results (Barreda-Ángeles et al., 2015; Li et al., 2022; Nonis et al., 2020). Barreda-Ángeles et al. (2015) examined physiological measures (electrodermal activity (EDA) and electromyography (EMG)) and three self-report measures (User Engagement Scale (UES), Computer System Usability Questionnaire (CSUQ) and International Positive and Negative Affect Schedule Short Form (I-PANAS-SF)) in an experimental search study that manipulated search response latency. While there were no significant differences in participants' self-reported experience, there were physiological differences in participants' reactions to different latency values.

Li et al. (2022) and Nonis et al. (2020) experienced similar issues triangulating self-reports and physiological measures. Li et al. (2022) used EEG to monitor participants' brain activity as they completed a 5-minute task with four different museum exhibition formats (game, 2D information kiosk, 3D and video) and self-reported their engagement with the UES-SF. Combining within-subject and paired comparison data, the authors concluded that there was correspondence between UES scores and EEG signals for medium and high engagement tasks, but conflicting findings for the least engaging task. Specifically, the EEG brain function network maps showed participants were paying less attention during this task although their self-reported engagement was high.

Nonis et al. (2020) trained a machine learning model using 750+ images of over 100 people expressing emotions (neutral, anger, disgust, fear, happiness, sadness, and surprise) to create facial depth maps revealing three classes of engagement: deactivation (low engagement; neutral expressions), average activation (medium engagement; happy, contented expressions), and activation (high engagement; surprise, embarrassment). The researchers then conducted a study with 24 young adults (20-30 years old), capturing facial expressions and self-reports using the original UES. UES scores were grouped as low, medium and high and applied to the facial depth maps. The authors examined the extent to which the UES and physiological method mapped to each other, finding correspondence for 14 of the 24 participants. The authors speculated that the lack of fit could be due to some participants reporting greater engagement than they felt, and other participants not recognizing some of their feelings during the reporting process.

Li et al. concluded that "relevant information will be lost in the study of user engagement if only questionnaires or interviews are used" (Li et al., 2022, p. 329). These studies suggest that triangulating self-reported engagement and physiological measures may be more challenging than finding synergy between self-reported engagement and behavior. One reason for this may be temporal differences in data collection. Edwards (2015) conducted a laboratory experiment to disambiguate user engagement and frustration. She observed that human physiology differed in the first 60 seconds of the task compared to the entire task and that physiological data is captured in the moment, whereas self-reported engagement is typically measured post-task or post-session and relies on the users' overall perceptions of the experience. Engagement is also (generally) more positive in nature and may be more challenging to capture physiologically than a more negative experience, i.e., frustration.

Chapter Summary

This chapter surveyed self-report, behavioral and physiological methods and measures used to study user engagement. It builds on prior work specific to the measurement of user engagement (Lalmas et al., 2014) and complements methodological work in the general social sciences, health psychology, and human-computer interaction fields.

Lalmas et al. (2014) predicted that the sensitivity of behavioral and physiological measures as signals of user engagement would increase, and that personalization would play a greater role in evaluating and predicting user engagement. This has certainly come to pass as illustrated in this chapter. While behavioral metrics were central in the designs of many of the studies profiled, it is worth noting that many researchers are using multiple methods to address their research questions. When it comes to evaluating user engagement, it is pragmatic to rely on a suite of methods rather than just one.

When selecting a methodological approach, we should remember that engagement is dependent on many things, including people's individual differences, needs, goals and preferences for interacting with technology, the features and affordances of the technology, and the alignment between these user and system factors (Lagan et al., 2020). We should also consider the financial and human constraints of the research situation, such as what equipment we have access to, our skills in using that equipment and analyzing the data we collect, and our ability to recruit representative participants. In addition, the measurement approach should be linked to how one wishes to apply what one learns. Specifically, Doherty and Doherty (2019) distinguish studies for obtaining a basic understanding of user engagement from those focused on developing autonomous systems that model and respond to users, and those that analyze patterns of use with specific technologies, including website, games and e-learning systems to inform design practices.

This chapter highlighted that all methods have their merits: self-reports provide a view into users' thoughts, ideas, feelings and perceptions; behavioral and physiological data show how experiences change in real time and over time. These types of methods can be used together to enhance researchers' ability to make sense of user engagement and triangulate different sources of data. Efforts to triangulate user engagement data have not always been successful, because different methods operative along different timescales, levels of granularity, etc. and direct comparisons between results are not feasible. Rather than arguing that one method or measure is better or more "objective" than another, a more productive approach is to be transparent about the methods used, how they fit the research question or context, and identify any limitations. Whatever method is used, employ it as robustly as possible.

References

Alserri, S. A., Zin, N. A. M., & Wook, T. S. M. T. (2019). Instrument validation for evaluating serious game engagement model. In *2019 International Conference on Electrical Engineering and Informatics (ICEEI)* (pp. 170–175). https://doi.org/10.1109/ICEEI47359.2019.8988873

Andrade, A. Q., Beleigoli, A. M. R., Silva, T. M. S., de Fátima, H., Diniz, M., & Ribeiro, A. L. P. (2019). Exploring the user engagement scale short form as a determinant of adherence in digital health interventions. *Studies in Health Technology and Informatics, 264*, 1901–1902. https://doi.org/10.3233/SHTI190704

Arguello, J., & Crescenzi, A. (2019). Using principal component analysis to better understand behavioral measures and their effects. *Proceedings of the 2019 ACM SIGIR International Conference on Theory of Information Retrieval* (pp. 177–184). https://doi.org/10.1145/3341981.3344222

Arguello, J., & Choi, B. (2019). The effects of working memory, perceptual speed, and inhibition in aggregated search. *ACM Transactions on Information Systems, 37*(3), 1–34. https://doi.org/10.1145/3322128

Astleitner, H. (2020). Handling validity problems in developmental measurement approaches—A confirmatory factor analysis approach on student engagement. In H. Astleitner (Ed.), *Intervention research in educational practice* (pp. 109–125). Waxmann Verlag.

Baker, R. S. J. d., D'Mello, S. K., Rodrigo, Ma. M. T., & Graesser, A. C. (2010). Better to be frustrated than bored: The incidence, persistence, and impact of learners' cognitive–affective states during interactions with three different computer-based learning environments. *International Journal of Human-Computer Studies, 68*(4), 223–241. https://doi.org/10.1016/j.ijhcs.2009.12.003

Barreda-Ángeles, M., Arapakis, I., Bai, X., Cambazoglu, B. B., & Pereda-Baños, A. (2015). Unconscious physiological effects of search latency on users and their click behaviour. *Proceedings of the 38th International ACM SIGIR Conference on Research and Development in Information Retrieval* (pp. 203–212). https://doi.org/10.1145/2766462.2767719

Bødker, S., Dindler, C., Iversen, O. S., & Smith, R. C. (2022). *Participatory design.* Springer Nature.

Carlton, J., Brown, A., Jay, C., & Keane, J. (2019). Inferring user engagement from interaction data. In *Extended Abstracts of the 2019 CHI Conference on Human Factors in Computing Systems* (pp. 1–6). https://doi.org/10.1145/3290607.3313009

Carlton, J., Brown, A., Jay, C., & Keane, J. (2021). Using interaction data to predict engagement with interactive media. *Proceedings of the 29th ACM International Conference on Multimedia* (pp. 1258–1266). https://doi.org/10.1145/3474085.3475631

Carrino, S., Caon, M., Khaled, O. A., & Mugellini, E. (2017). Investigating how to measure mobile user engagement. In P. Perego, G. Andreoni, & G. Rizzo (Eds.), *Wireless mobile communication and healthcare* (pp. 38–44). Springer International Publishing. https://doi.org/10.1007/978-3-319-58877-3_5

Castiblanco Jimenez, I. A., Nonis, F., Olivetti, E. C., Ulrich, L., Moos, S., Monaci, M. G., Marcolin, F., & Vezzetti, E. (2023). Exploring user engagement in museum scenario with EEG—A case study in MAV craftsmanship museum in Valle d'Aosta Region, Italy. *Electronics, 12*(18), 3810. https://doi.org/10.3390/electronics12183810

Chen, A. T., Wu, S., Tomasino, K. N., Lattie, E. G., & Mohr, D. C. (2019). A multi-faceted approach to characterizing user behavior and experience in a digital mental health intervention. *Journal of Biomedical Informatics, 94*, 103187. https://doi.org/10.1016/j.jbi.2019.103187

Chong, D. (2021, September 24). *Deep dive into Netflix's recommender system.* Medium. https://towardsdatascience.com/deep-dive-into-netflixs-recommender-system-341806ae3b48

Connaway, L. S., & Radford, M. L. (2021). *Individual and focus group interviews. Research methods in library and information science.* Bloomsbury Publishing USA.

Cunningham, T., Pandey, S., Sigerson, L., Stray, J., Allen, J., Barrilleaux, B., Iyer, R., Milli, S., Kothari, M., & Rezaei, B. (2024). *What we know about using non-engagement signals in content ranking* (arXiv:2402.06831). arXiv. https://doi.org/10.48550/arXiv.2402.06831

De Carolis, B., D'Errico, F., Macchiarulo, N., & Palestra, G. (2019). Engaged faces: measuring and monitoring student engagement from face and gaze behavior. *IEEE/WIC/ACM International Conference on Web Intelligence—Companion Volume* (pp. 80–85). https://doi.org/10.1145/3358695.3361748

Deng, S., Jiang, Y., Li, H., & Liu, Y. (2020). Who contributes what? Scrutinizing the activity data of 4.2 million Zhihu users via immersion scores. *Information Processing and Management, 57*(5), 102274. https://doi.org/10.1016/j.ipm.2020.102274

DeVellis, R. F. (2003). *Scale development: Theory and applications* (4th edn). SAGE Publications, Inc.

Dogan, E., Sander, C., Wagner, X., Hegerl, U., & Kohls, E. (2017). Smartphone-based monitoring of objective and subjective data in affective disorders: Where are we and where are we going? Systematic review. *Journal of Medical Internet Research, 19*(7), e262. https://doi.org/10.2196/jmir.7006

Doherty, K., & Doherty, G. (2019). Engagement in HCI: Conception, theory and measurement. *ACM Computing Surveys, 51*(5), 1–39. https://doi.org/10.1145/3234149

Edwards, A. (2015). *Engaged or frustrated? Disambiguating engagement and frustration in search* [Ph.D., The University of North Carolina at Chapel Hill]. https://www.proquest.com/docview/1805320052/abstract/5BA56E0AA1704B08PQ/1

Ericsson, K. A., & Simon, H. A. (1984). In *Protocol analysis: Verbal reports as data.* MIT Press.

Ericsson, K. A., & Simon, H. A. (1980). Verbal reports as data. *Psychological Review, 87*(3), 215–251. https://doi.org/10.1037/0033-295X.87.3.215

Fontaine, G., Cossette, S., Maheu-Cadotte, M.-A., Mailhot, T., Lavoie, P., Gagnon, M.-P., Dubé, V., & Côté, J. (2020). Traduction, adaptation et évaluation psychométrique préliminaire d'une mesure d'engagement et d'une mesure de charge cognitive en contexte d'apprentissage numérique. *Pédagogie Médicale, 20*(2), 79–90. https://doi.org/10.1051/pmed/2020009

Gabrielli, S., Rizzi, S., Bassi, G., Carbone, S., Maimone, R., Marchesoni, M., & Forti, S. (2021). Engagement and effectiveness of a healthy-coping intervention via Chatbot for university students during the COVID-19 pandemic: Mixed methods proof-of-concept study. *JMIR mHealth and uHealth, 9*(5), e27965. https://doi.org/10.2196/27965

Georges, V., Courtemanche, F., Fredette, M., & Doyon-Poulin, P. (2020). Emotional maps for user experience research in the wild. In *Extended Abstracts of the 2020 CHI Conference on Human Factors in Computing Systems* (pp. 1–8). https://doi.org/10.1145/3334480.3383042

Goetzen, A., Wang, R., Redmiles, E. M., Zannettou, S., & Ayalon, O. (2023). *Likes and fragments: Examining perceptions of time spent on TikTok* (arXiv:2303.02041). arXiv. http://arxiv.org/abs/2303.02041

Gomez-Uribe, C. A., & Hunt, N. (2016). The Netflix recommender system: Algorithms, business value, and innovation. *ACM Transactions on Management Information Systems, 6*(4), 1–19. https://doi.org/10.1145/2843948

Grinberg, N. (2018). Identifying modes of user engagement with online news and their relationship to information gain in text. *Proceedings of the 2018 World Wide Web Conference on World Wide Web—WWW '18* (pp. 1745–1754). https://doi.org/10.1145/3178876.3186180

Gunawardena, N., Ginige, J. A., & Javadi, B. (2022). Eye-tracking technologies in mobile devices using edge computing: A systematic review. *ACM Computing Surveys, 55*(8), 33.

Hallifax, S. (2020). *Adaptive gamification of digital learning environments.* [Doctoral Dissertation]. Université Jean Moulin Lyon 3.

Harari, G., & Gosling, S. (2023). Understanding behaviours in context using mobile sensing. *Nature Reviews Psychology, 2.* https://doi.org/10.1038/s44159-023-00235-3

Holdener, M., Gut, A., & Angerer, A. (2020). Applicability of the user engagement scale to mobile health: A survey-based quantitative study. *JMIR mHealth and uHealth, 8*(1), e13244. https://doi.org/10.2196/13244

How does Oura Ring work: Smart Ring Health Tracking. (n.d.). Oura Ring. Retrieved July 5, 2024, from https://ouraring.com

Kelders, S. M., Kip, H., & Greeff, J. (2020). Psychometric evaluation of the TWente engagement with Ehealth technologies scale (TWEETS): Evaluation study. *Journal of Medical Internet Research, 22*(10), e17757. https://doi.org/10.2196/17757

Kelly, D. (2009). Methods for evaluating interactive information retrieval systems with users. *Foundations and Trends in Information Retrieval, 3*(1–2), 1–224. https://doi.org/10.1561/1500000012

Klein, R. M., Vallis, E. H., & Chisholm, J. D. (2019). A comparison of engagement between the attention network test and a videogame-like version, called the attention trip. *International Journal of Human-Computer Interaction, 35*(19), 1813–1819. https://doi.org/10.1080/10447318.2019.1574058

Koç, D. (2024, January 10). Top 20 user engagement metrics to track and measure. *Storyly.* Retrieved, https://www.storyly.io/post/top-user-engagement-metrics-to-track-and-measure#customer-lifetime-value-clv

Ksibi, A., Alluhaidan, A. S. D., Salhi, A., & El-Rahman, S. A. (2021). Overview of lifelogging: Current challenges and advances. *IEEE Access, 9,* 62630–62641. https://doi.org/10.1109/ACCESS.2021.3073469

Kunze, K., Sanchez, S., Dingler, T., Augereau, O., Kise, K., Inami, M., & Tsutomu, T. (2015). The augmented narrative: Toward estimating reader engagement. In *Proceedings of the 6th Augmented Human International Conference* (pp. 163–164). https://doi.org/10.1145/2735711.2735814

Lagan, S., Aquino, P., Emerson, M. R., Fortuna, K., Walker, R., & Torous, J. (2020). Actionable health app evaluation: Translating expert frameworks into objective metrics. *Npj Digital Medicine, 3*(1), 1–8. https://doi.org/10.1038/s41746-020-00312-4

Lallé, S., Conati, C., & Carenini, G. (2017). Impact of individual differences on user experience with a real-world visualization interface for public engagement. In *Proceedings of the 25th Conference on User Modeling, Adaptation and Personalization* (pp. 369–370). https://doi.org/10.1145/307 9628.3079634

Lallemand, C., & Koenig, V. (2020). Measuring the contextual dimension of user experience: Development of the user experience context scale (UXCS). In *Proceedings of the 11th Nordic Conference on Human-Computer Interaction: Shaping Experiences, Shaping Society* (pp. 1–13). https://doi.org/10.1145/3419249.3420156

Lalmas, M., O'Brien, H., & Yom-Tov, E. (2014). Measuring user engagement. In *Synthesis Lectures on Information Concepts, Retrieval, and Services* (Vol. 6). https://doi.org/10.2200/S00605ED1 V01Y201410ICR038

Landa-Avila, I. C., & Cruz, M.-L. (2017). Engagement in a virtual reality game with gesture hand interface. An empirical evaluation of user engagement scale (UES). In A. Marcus & W. Wang (Eds.), *Design, user experience, and usability: Designing pleasurable experiences* (pp. 414–427). Springer International Publishing. https://doi.org/10.1007/978-3-319-58637-3_33

Li, J., Sun, C., Xanat, V. M., & Ochiai, Y. (2022). Electroencephalography and self-assessment evaluation of engagement with online exhibitions: Case study of google arts and culture. *International Conference on Human-Computer Interaction*, (pp. 316–331).

Loeffler, J. (2021, May 18). *Google's new photo technology is creepy as hell—and seriously problematic*. TechRadar. https://www.techradar.com/news/googles-new-photo-technology-is-creepy-af-and-seriously-problematic

Martinez-Comeche, J.-A., & Ruthven, I. (2021). Engaging interaction and long-term engagement with WhatsApp in an everyday life context: Exploratory study. *Journal of Documentation, 77*(4), 825–850. https://doi.org/10.1108/JD-07-2020-0115

McCay-Peet, L., Toms, E. G., & Kelloway, E. K. (2014). *Development and assessment of the content validity of a scale to measure how well a digital environment facilitates serendipity*. https://informationr.net/ir/19-3/paper630.html

McDaniel, B. T., Pater, J., Cornet, V., Mughal, S., Reining, L., Schaller, A., Radesky, J., & Drouin, M. (2023). Parents' desire to change phone use: Associations with objective smartphone use and feelings about problematic use and distraction. *Computers in Human Behavior, 148*, 107907. https://doi.org/10.1016/j.chb.2023.107907

Mehrabi, N., Morstatter, F., Saxena, N., Lerman, K., & Galstyan, A. (2022). *A survey on bias and fairness in machine learning* (arXiv:1908.09635). arXiv. https://doi.org/10.48550/arXiv.1908.09635

Michie, S., Yardley, L., West, R., Patrick, K., & Greaves, F. (2017). Developing and evaluating digital interventions to promote behavior change in health and health care: Recommendations resulting from an international workshop. *Journal of Medical Internet Research, 19*(6), e232. https://doi.org/10.2196/jmir.7126

Milli, S., Belli, L., & Hardt, M. (2021). From optimizing engagement to measuring value. *Proceedings of the 2021 ACM Conference on Fairness, Accountability, and Transparency* (pp. 714–722). https://doi.org/10.1145/3442188.3445933

Miranda, D., Li, C., & Darin, T. (2021). UES-Br: Translation and cross-cultural adaptation of the user engagement scale for Brazilian Portuguese. *Proceedings of the ACM on Human-Computer Interaction, 5*(CHI PLAY), 1–22. https://doi.org/10.1145/3474705

Mostafa, J., & Gwizdka, J. (2016). Deepening the role of the user: Neuro-physiological evidence as a basis for studying and improving search. *Proceedings of the 2016 ACM on Conference on Human Information Interaction and Retrieval* (pp. 63–70). https://doi.org/10.1145/2854946.2854979

Nahum-Shani, I., Smith, S. N., Spring, B. J., Collins, L. M., Witkiewitz, K., Tewari, A., & Murphy, S. A. (2018). Just-in-time adaptive interventions (JITAIs) in mobile health: Key components and design principles for ongoing health behavior support. *Annals of Behavioral Medicine, 52*(6), 446–462. https://doi.org/10.1007/s12160-016-9830-8

Navarro, D., Sundstedt, V., & Garro, V. (2021). Biofeedback methods in entertainment video games: A review of physiological interaction techniques. *Proceedings of the ACM on Human-Computer Interaction, 5*(CHI PLAY), 268:1-268:32. https://doi.org/10.1145/3474695

Nonis, F., Olivetti, E. C., Marcolin, F., Violante, M. G., Vezzetti, E., & Moos, S. (2020). Questionnaires or inner feelings: Who measures the engagement better? *Applied Sciences, 10*(2), 609. https://doi.org/10.3390/app10020609

Novák, J. Š, Masner, J., Benda, P., Šimek, P., & Merunka, V. (2023). Eye tracking, usability, and user experience: A systematic review. *International Journal of Human-Computer Interaction.* https://doi.org/10.1080/10447318.2023.2221600

O'Brien, H. L. (2016). Translating theory into methodological practice. In H. O'Brien & P. Cairns (Eds.), *Why engagement matters: Cross-disciplinary perspectives of user engagement in digital media* (pp. 27–52). Springer Cham.

O'Brien, H. L., & Cairns, P. (2015). An empirical evaluation of the user engagement scale (UES) in online news environments. *Information Processing and Management, 51*(4), 413–427. https://doi.org/10.1016/j.ipm.2015.03.003

O'Brien, H. L., & Lebow, M. (2013). Mixed-methods approach to measuring user experience in online news interactions. *Journal of the American Society for Information Science and Technology, 64*(8), 1543–1556. https://doi.org/10.1002/asi.22871

O'Brien, H. L., & Toms, E. (2010). The development and evaluation of a survey to measure user engagement. *Journal of the American Society for Information Science and Technology, 61*(1), 50–69. https://doi.org/10.1002/asi.21229

O'Brien, H. L., & Toms, E. G. (2013). Examining the generalizability of the user engagement scale (UES) in exploratory search. *Information Processing and Management, 49*(5), 1092–1107. https://doi.org/10.1016/j.ipm.2012.08.005

O'Brien, H. L., Cairns, P., & Hall, M. (2018). A practical approach to measuring user engagement with the refined user engagement scale (UES) and new UES short form. *International Journal of Human-Computer Studies, 112,* 28–39. https://doi.org/10.1016/j.ijhcs.2018.01.004

O'Brien, H. L., Arguello, J., & Capra, R. (2020a). An empirical study of interest, task complexity, and search behaviour on user engagement. *Information Processing and Management, 57*(3), 102226.

O'Brien, H. L., Morton, E., Kampen, A., Barnes, S. J., & Michalak, E. E. (2020b). Beyond clicks and downloads: A call for a more comprehensive approach to measuring mobile-health app engagement. *Bjpsych Open, 6*(5), e86. https://doi.org/10.1192/bjo.2020.72

O'Brien, H. L., Roll, I., Kampen, A., & Davoudi, N. (2022). Rethinking (Dis)engagement in human-computer interaction. *Computers in Human Behavior, 128,* 107109. https://doi.org/10.1016/j.chb.2021.107109

O'Brien, H. L, & McCay-Peet, L. (2017). Asking "Good" questions: Questionnaire design and analysis in interactive information retrieval research. In *Proceedings of the 2017 Conference on Conference Human Information Interaction and Retrieval (CHIIR '17)* (pp. 27–36). https://doi.org/10.1145/3020165.3020167

O'Brien, H. L., Chen, A. T., Kaneshiro, J., & Zaslavsky, O. (2024). Designing for digital health engagement: Lessons learned from the virtual online communities for aging life experience (VOCALE) intervention. *Interacting with Computers,* iwae030. https://doi.org/10.1093/iwc/iwae030

O'Brien, H. L. (2008). *Defining and measuring engagement in user experiences with technology* [Doctoral Dissertation]. Dalhousie University.

Oura Ring. Smart Ring for Fitness, Stress, Sleep and Health. (n.d.). Oura Ring. Retrieved July 5, 2024, from https://ouraring.com

Oxford English Dictionary. (2007). *questionnaire, n. Meanings, etymology and more | Oxford English Dictionary.* Dictionary. https://www.oed.com/dictionary/questionnaire_n

Perugia, G., Díaz-Boladeras, M., Català-Mallofré, A., Barakova, E. I., & Rauterberg, M. (2022). ENGAGE-DEM: A model of engagement of people with dementia. *IEEE Transactions on Affective Computing, 13*(2), 926–943. https://doi.org/10.1109/TAFFC.2020.2980275

Peterson, R. (2000). In *Constructing effective questionnaires.* SAGE Publications, Inc. https://doi.org/10.4135/9781483349022

Pham, Q., Graham, G., Carrion, C., Morita, P. P., Seto, E., Stinson, J. N., & Cafazzo, J. A. (2019). A library of analytic indicators to evaluate effective engagement with consumer mHealth apps for chronic conditions: Scoping review. *JMIR mHealth and uHealth, 7*(1), e11941. https://doi.org/10.2196/11941

Ponciano, L., & Brasileiro, F. (2014). Finding volunteers' engagement profiles in human computatin for citizen science projects. *Human Computation, 1*(2), 247–266.

Puntha, P., Jitanugoon, S., & Lee, P.-C. (2021). Engagement on social networks during the COVID-19 pandemic: A comparison among healthcare professionals, fitness influencers, and healthy food influencers. *The 8th Multidisciplinary International Social Networks Conference* (pp. 5–14). https://doi.org/10.1145/3504006.3504008

Ramírez-Moreno, M. A., Keshtkar, S., Padilla-Reyes, D. A., Ramos-López, E., García-Martínez, M., Hernández-Luna, M. C., Mogro, A. E., Mahlknecht, J., Huertas, J. I., Peimbert-García, R. E., et al. (2021). Sensors for sustainable smart cities: A review. *Applied Sciences, 11*(17), 8198. https://doi.org/10.3390/app11178198

Rivera, Y. M., Moran, M. B., Thrul, J., Joshu, C., & Smith, K. C. (2022). Contextualizing engagement with health information on Facebook: Using the social media content and context elicitation method. *Journal of Medical Internet Research.* https://www.proquest.com/scholarly-journals/contextualizing-engagement-with-health/docview/2645698379/se-2

Ross, C. S. (1999). Finding without seeking: The information encounter in the context of reading for pleasure. *Information Processing and Management, 35*(6), 783–799. https://doi.org/10.1016/S0306-4573(99)00026-6

Said, F. F., & Çarçani, K. (2020). Exploring engagement in distributed meetings during COVID-19 lock-down. *Proceedings of the Thirteenth International Conference on Advances in Computer-Human Interactions* (pp. 104–112).

Sanatkar, S., Baldwin, P. A., Huckvale, K., Clarke, J., Christensen, H., Harvey, S., & Proudfoot, J. (2019). Using cluster analysis to explore engagement and e-attainment as emergent behavior in electronic mental health. *Journal of Medical Internet Research, 21*(11), e14728. https://doi.org/10.2196/14728

Schrepp, M. (2020). A comparison of UX questionnaires-what is their underlying concept of user experience? *Mensch Und Computer 2020-Workshopband.*

Shao, Z., Zhao, R., Yuan, S., Ding, M., & Wang, Y. (2022). Tracing the evolution of AI in the past decade and forecasting the emerging trends. *Expert Systems with Applications, 209*, 118221. https://doi.org/10.1016/j.eswa.2022.118221

Shiri, A., & Stobbs, R. (2018). Community-driven user evaluation of the Inuvialuit cultural heritage digital library. *Proceedings of the Association for Information Science and Technology, 55*(1), 440–449. https://doi.org/10.1002/pra2.2018.14505501048

Syn, S. Y. (2016). What do users see when health information with different levels of sensitivity is presented on Facebook?: Preliminary findings with eye tracking techniques: What do users see when health information with different levels of sensitivity is presented on Facebook?: Preliminary findings with eye tracking techn. *Proceedings of the Association for Information Science and Technology, 53*(1), 1–4. https://doi.org/10.1002/pra2.2016.14505301149

Syn, S. Y. (2021). Health information communication during a pandemic crisis: Analysis of CDC Facebook Page during COVID-19. *Online Information Review, 45*(4), 672–686. https://doi.org/10.1108/OIR-09-2020-0416

Tang, X., Liu, Y., Shah, N., Shi, X., Mitra, P., & Wang, S. (2020). Knowing your FATE: Friendship, action and temporal explanations for user engagement prediction on social apps. *Proceedings of the 26th ACM SIGKDD International Conference on Knowledge Discovery and Data Mining* (pp. 2269–2279). https://doi.org/10.1145/3394486.3403276

Thomas, P., O'Brien, H., & Rowlands, T. (2016). Measuring engagement with online forms. *Proceedings of the 2016 ACM on Conference on Human Information Interaction and Retrieval* (pp. 325–328). https://doi.org/10.1145/2854946.2854988

Tian, X., Wiggins, J. B., Fahid, F. M., Emerson, A., Bounajim, D., Smith, A., Boyer, K. E., Wiebe, E., Mott, B., & Lester, J. (2021). Modeling frustration trajectories and problem-solving behaviors in adaptive learning environments for introductory computer science. In I. Roll, D. McNamara, S. Sosnovsky, R. Luckin, & V. Dimitrova (Eds.), *Artificial intelligence in education* (Vol. 12749, pp. 355–360). Springer International Publishing. https://doi.org/10.1007/978-3-030-78270-2_63

Tian, Y., Zhou, K., & Pelleg, D. (2021). What and how long: Prediction of mobile app engagement. *ACM Transactions on Information Systems, 40*(1). https://doi.org/10.1145/3464301

Torous, J., Michalak, E. E., & O'Brien, H. L. (2020). Digital health and engagement—Looking behind the measures and methods. *JAMA Network Open, 3*(7), e2010918–e2010918. https://doi.org/10.1001/jamanetworkopen.2020.10918

Trifan, A., Oliveira, M., & Oliveira, J. L. (2019). Passive sensing of health outcomes through smartphones: Systematic review of current solutions and possible limitations. *JMIR mHealth and uHealth, 7*(8), e12649. https://doi.org/10.2196/12649

Vassio, L., Garetto, M., Chiasserini, C., & Leonardi, E. (2021). Temporal dynamics of posts and user engagement of influencers on Facebook and Instagram. *Proceedings of the 2021 IEEE/ACM International Conference on Advances in Social Networks Analysis and Mining* (pp. 129–133). https://doi.org/10.1145/3487351.3488340

Wei, Y., Zheng, P., Deng, H., Wang, X., Li, X., & Fu, H. (2020). Design features for improving mobile health intervention user engagement: Systematic review and thematic analysis. *Journal of Medical Internet Research, 22*(12), e21687. https://doi.org/10.2196/21687

Wiebe, E. N., Lamb, A., Hardy, M., & Sharek, D. (2014). Measuring engagement in video game-based environments: Investigation of the user engagement scale. *Computers in Human Behavior, 32*, 123–132. https://doi.org/10.1016/j.chb.2013.12.001

Wu, Y., Liu, Y., Tsai, Y.-H.R., & Yau, S.-T. (2019). Investigating the role of eye movements and physiological signals in search satisfaction prediction using geometric analysis. *Journal of the Association for Information Science and Technology, 70*(9), 981–999.

Wu, S. (2021). *Measuring collective attention in online content: sampling, engagement, and network effects* [PhD Thesis, The Australian National University]. Available from ProQuest Dissertations & Theses Global. (2600829449).

Yardley, L., Spring, B. J., Riper, H., Morrison, L. G., Crane, D. H., Curtis, K., Merchant, G. C., Naughton, F., & Blandford, A. (2016). Understanding and promoting effective engagement with digital behavior change interventions. *American Journal of Preventive Medicine, 51*(5), 833–842. https://doi.org/10.1016/j.amepre.2016.06.015

Ye, Z., Xie, X., Ai, Q., Liu, Y., Wang, Z., Su, W., & Zhang, M. (2024). Relevance feedback with brain signals. *ACM Transactions on Information Systems, 42*(4), 93:1–93:37. https://doi.org/10.1145/3637874

Yeager, C. M., & Benight, C. C. (2018). If we build it, will they come? Issues of engagement with digital health interventions for trauma recovery. *mHealth, 4*, 37–37.

Zhao, C. Y., Lian, J., Song, S., & Ying, J. (2022). Engaging with immersive technologies in medical library: An investigation of students' perceived affordances and constraints. *ACM SIGIR Conference on Human Information Interaction and Retrieval* (pp. 277–283). https://doi.org/10.1145/349 8366.3505827

Zhou, Y., Calder, B. J., Malthouse, E. C., & Hessary, Y. K. (2021). Not all clicks are equal: Detecting engagement with digital content. *Journal of Media Business Studies*, 1–18.

Zhuang, M., Toms, E. G., & Demartini, G. (2016). The relationship between user perception and user behaviour in interactive information retrieval evaluation. *Advances in Information Retrieval* (pp. 293–305). https://doi.org/10.1007/978-3-319-30671-1_22

Zhuang, M., Demartini, G., & Toms, E. G. (2017). Understanding engagement through search behaviour. *Proceedings of the 2017 ACM on Conference on Information and Knowledge Management* (pp. 1957–1966). https://doi.org/10.1145/3132847.3132978

Zhuang, M. (2016). Modelling user search behaviour based on process. *Proceedings of the 39th International ACM SIGIR Conference on Research and Development in Information Retrieval* (pp. 1179). https://doi.org/10.1145/2911451.2911486

Zuckerman, E., & McGrady, R. (2024, June 27). *AI companies train language models on YouTube's archive—making family-and-friends videos a privacy risk*. The Conversation. http://theconversation.com/ai-companies-train-language-models-on-youtubes-archive-making-family-and-friends-videos-a-privacy-risk-23212

Conclusion

6

This synthesis brought together select literature to tell the story of user engagement past and present. In Chap. 1, I reviewed definitions of user engagement and described some of the systems that would be discussed in this book about digital engagement. Chapter 2 provided an orientation to specific theories and models of user engagement, emphasizing the importance of conceptually situating our understanding and study of engagement to guide the design and interpretation of research, communicate findings, and investigate changes in user engagement over time. Chapter 3 focused on the intersection of people, information, and technology in bringing about engaging interactions. I reviewed studies that explored different facets of users (e.g., demographics, cognitive processes), content (genre, format, structure, paralinguistic cues, sentiment, polarity, comprehension and trust), tasks (topic, complexity) and systems (storytelling, interactivity, search clarification and discovery) in relation to engagement. This chapter was followed by Chap. 4, which broadened the people-information-technology triad by discussing persuasive technologies and gamification that have impacted how we engage with information systems; this chapter also explored the implications of design on active and passive engagement using TikTok as an example. Finally, Chap. 5 provided an overview of self-report, behavioral and physiological measures. While these methods are not new to the study of engagement, increasingly sophisticated technologies are opening new possibilities for the unobtrusive observation of user behaviors and physiology, as well as the transformation of behavioral and physiological signals to make predictions about what, when, and how we will engage with technologies.

This book represents a snapshot of current perspectives on user engagement research and practice. A recurring theme in all chapters has been the metamorphosis of engagement over the past 20 years from a multidimensional, experiential construct to a

H. O'Brien, *User Engagement Research and Practice*, Synthesis Lectures on Information Concepts, Retrieval, and Services, https://doi.org/10.1007/978-3-031-80916-3_6

metric of user attention and activity that is driving the design of digital systems. Because of this connection, user engagement has taken on negative connotations in many spaces, including discussions about the physical and mental harms of technology use across the lifespan, polarization and the spread of mis/disinformation, and social media regulation (Center for Human Technology, 2021; UNESCO, 2024). Undoubtedly, user engagement is central in conversations we need to have about the future of technology, and it is entangled within the political, social and economic systems that (in)form the digital ecosystem. These systems are comprised of many stakeholders, some of whom hold more power than others.

I have wondered over the past few years whether I should continue to study user engagement. When I started my doctoral work, I was thinking only about the positive implications of engagement, how it could be used to support outcomes like learning or make challenging things like investing effort in a complex information search a bit more palatable. This was obviously very naive on my part! It is unlikely that we will all go back to using flip phones or that new technologies like generative AI will go back in the box. So, what now? What is the future of user engagement?

In the following I share what could be considered "grand challenges" for researchers in this area. These grand challenges involve normalizing disengagement; encouraging transparency; treating information critically; and prioritizing privacy and ethics.

6.1   Normalizing Disengagement

One of the main challenges with current conceptualizations of user engagement is that we must always be 'on'. Rather than lamenting that disengagement is "the lowest levels of affective, cognitive and behavioural engagement for individuals or groups" (Johnston, 2018, p. 22), we could embrace it. Nahum-Shani et al. (2018) and others describe technology-induced "fatigue," or how constant engagement leads to "weariness" and "burnout," reducing people's motivation (p. 450). This example reinforces why notions of quantity over quality are inadequate to serve experiential needs and promote agentic (re)engagement. We need to "make space for disengagement" by allowing people to pause or stop engaging in alignment with their goals and needs, and to return to devices or applications as/when desired (O'Brien et al., 2022). Engagement and disengagement are not dichotomous; rather they are natural parts of technology use, and both should be supported in the design of digital tools. Helping users maintain control over their interactions moves us away from "engagement-for-engagement's-sake" and toward more meaningful outcomes for technology users.

6.2   Encouraging Transparency

Some of the studies featured in this book have tried to use engagement to help people make more informed decisions about the technologies they are using or their information interaction processes (e.g., Kitkowska et al., 2022; Rossel, 2020; Scott, 2022; Sekulić et al., 2021). Along with transparency, options for "opting out" must be developed that do not force people to enter new digital spaces or be excluded from essential services (Kuntsman & Miyake, 2022). Transparency can be "top down" and brought about by regulators or developers, but it can also be bottom-up. In their ethnographic study of TikTok, Schellewald (2021) highlighted "meta" videos that "start talking about how Tik-Tok's algorithms place content in your feed from users that have similar interests or who are in a similar life situation" (p. 1449–1450). These "speedbumps" create friction in the viewing experience to prompt pause and reflection and show that platform users can be empowered to advocate for transparency.

6.3   Treating Information Critically

Characteristics of information content are meaningful for engagement (Chap. 3), but content is also used to persuade (Chap. 4). In addition to designing more transparent technologies, how we design *information* also has implications. Jia and Sundar (2023) successfully experimented with interactive visualizations to increase participants' curiosity and interest in base rate information and decrease their cognitive load. Base rate information shows the status of an issue rather than focusing on a single case (i.e., exemplifying information), which may be rare and misleading, but tends to garner more attention. Supporting base rate information presentation may be one way to design information for deeper, evidence-based information processing and to promote critical literacy.

Critical literacy in the current technology landscape also means acknowledging the limitations of existing tactics (e.g., fact checking) and deploying new strategies that emphasize the self, the medium and their intersection (Cho et al., 2024). Cho et al. suggest that this involves moving beyond content to the values embedded within it and distinguishing personal values from those of content creators and distributors.

> Users should be aware of the multiplicity and malleability of realities on social media. A social media literate person demonstrates an awareness of the multiple criteria with which people assess realism and the pitfalls of relying on personal, emotional resonance, and perceived internal consistency of a social media message for realism judgments...users should be provided with tools and resources to understand the lived experiences through which the misinformation is interpreted, accepted, and internalized, as well as the values and worldviews that propel the production and dissemination of misinformation. (Cho et al., 2024, p. 953)

At the same time, recognition that different skills might be needed to critically engage with similar content across multiple platforms encourages a more dynamic approach to literacy (Swart, 2023). There may also be opportunities to promote more critical reflection on the datafication of our own information and technology use practices (Busch & McCarthy, 2021). This might involve thinking about whether the risks of technologies that tailor our information worlds are truly worth the benefits.

6.4   Prioritizing Privacy and Ethical Treatment of Data

Privacy and ethics have not been explicitly discussed in earlier chapters, but they are certainly in the background. Without reams of user data, systems cannot make reliable predictions about user behavior and algorithms cannot tailor and customize content to user needs. This data is often collected through terms of use that people do not read and may be too complex to understand. Sometimes these terms and conditions are breached.

For instance, in 2022, the Office of the Privacy Commissioner of Canada issued a statement about the outcome of federal and provincial investigations into the Tim Hortons' app. Tim Horton's is a popular restaurant chain with over 1500 locations that has been serving "double doubles"[1] for over 50 years; it is also a major contributor to community initiatives, especially youth camps and sport (*Tim Hortons*, n.d.). According to the Privacy Commissioners' report:

> The Tim Hortons app asked for permission to access the mobile device's geolocation functions, but misled many users to believe information would only be accessed when the app was in use. In reality, the app tracked users as long as the device was on, continually collecting their location data.
>
> The app also used location data to infer where users lived, where they worked, and whether they were travelling. It generated an "event" every time users entered or left a Tim Hortons competitor, a major sports venue, or their home or workplace.
>
> Location data is highly sensitive because it can be used to infer where people live and work, reveal trips to medical clinics. It can be used to make deductions about religious beliefs, sexual preferences, social political affiliations and more. (Office of the Privacy Commissioner of Canada, 2022)

This example is not just about the mismanagement of personal data. It is also about what companies choose to collect about people. This approach to data collection promotes a "just in case" (we need it) or "just because" (we can, and might need it for something)

---

[1] "Double double" is shorthand for a coffee with two creams and two sugars. .

mentality, rather than asking what is beneficial and less risky for the end user.[2] As consumers and as researchers we should be questioning the just in case and just because collection of user data to optimize engagement.

The Internet and social media make it possible for both researchers and marketers to study social phenomenon with the idea that, if data is "publicly available" or if users consent to companies' terms and conditions, then their data is fair game. Notions of privacy and ethics must extend beyond this public versus private dichotomy to consider the individuals and communities whose data is targeted or exposed. Shifting our thinking away from engagement as *the* target would move us beyond optimizing attention to creating purposeful experiences for people who use technologies.

These challenges will not easily be addressed. However, it is hoped that thinking about these challenges will encourage readers to pursue more reflective and thoughtful approaches to user engagement, and be in dialogue with others who are advocating for more sustainable, transparent and responsible development and use of technologies.

References

Busch, P. A., & McCarthy, S. (2021). Antecedents and consequences of problematic smartphone use: A systematic literature review of an emerging research area. *Computers in Human Behavior, 114*, 106414. https://doi.org/10.1016/j.chb.2020.106414

Center for Human Technology. (2021, June). *Ledger of Harms*. https://ledger.humanetech.com/

Cho, H., Cannon, J., Lopez, R., & Li, W. (2024). Social media literacy: A conceptual framework. *New Media and Society, 26*(2), 941–960. https://doi.org/10.1177/14614448211068530

Tim Hortons. (n.d.). Retrieved 5 July 2024, from https://www.timhortons.ca

Jia, H., & Sundar, S. S. (2023). Vivid and engaging: Effects of interactive data visualization on perceptions and attitudes about social issues. *Digital Journalism*, 1–25. https://doi.org/10.1080/21670811.2023.2250815

Johnston, K. A. (2018). Toward a Theory of social engagement. In K. A. Johnston & M. Taylor (Eds.), *The handbook of communication engagement* (pp. 17–32). Wiley & Sons, Inc. https://doi.org/10.1002/9781119167600.ch2

Kitkowska, A., Högberg, J., & Wästlund, E. (2022). Online terms and conditions: Improving user engagement, awareness, and satisfaction through UI design. *CHI Conference on Human Factors in Computing Systems* (pp. 1–22). https://doi.org/10.1145/3491102.3517720

Kuntsman, A., & Miyake, E. (2022). *Paradoxes of digital disengagement: In search of the opt-out button*. University of Westminster Press. https://doi.org/10.16997/book61

Nahum-Shani, I., Smith, S. N., Spring, B. J., Collins, L. M., Witkiewitz, K., Tewari, A., & Murphy, S. A. (2018). Just-in-time adaptive interventions (JITAIs) in mobile health: Key components and design principles for ongoing health behavior support. *Annals of Behavioral Medicine, 52*(6), 446–462. https://doi.org/10.1007/s12160-016-9830-8

---

[2] This is labelled "behavioral surplus" by Zuboff (2018), who traces Google's evolution from collecting user data to learn from searchers and improve search functionality to generating ad revenue. Zuboff argues that this moved search away from the use of data as an investment in user experience to a means of surveillance.

O'Brien, H. L., Roll, I., Kampen, A., & Davoudi, N. (2022). Rethinking (Dis)engagement in human-computer interaction. *Computers in Human Behavior, 128,* 107109. https://doi.org/10.1016/j.chb.2021.107109

Office of the Privacy Commissioner of Canada. (2022, June 1). *News release: Tim Hortons app violated privacy laws in collection of 'vast amounts' of sensitive location data.* https://www.priv.gc.ca/en/opc-news/news-and-announcements/2022/nr-c_220601/

Rossel, F. (2020). *The influence of explanations in recommender systems on user engagement.* [Bachelor Thesis]. Jönköping University. . https://urn.kb.se/resolve?urn=urn:nbn:se:hj:diva-50373

Schellewald, A. (2021). Communicative forms on TikTok: Perspectives from digital ethnography. *International Journal of Communication, 15*(0), 1437–1457.

Scott, A. S. (2022). *Dynamic consent: A mechanism for engagement* [PhD Thesis]. University of Oxford.

Sekulić, I., Aliannejadi, M., & Crestani, F. (2021). *User engagement prediction for clarification in search* (arXiv:2102.04163). arXiv. http://arxiv.org/abs/2102.04163

Swart, J. (2023). Tactics of news literacy: How young people access, evaluate, and engage with news on social media. *New Media and Society, 25*(3), 505–521. https://doi.org/10.1177/14614448211011447

UNESCO Press Release. (2024, June 6). *Online disinformation: UNESCO unveils action plan to regulate social media platforms | UNESCO.* UNESCO Press Release. https://www.unesco.org/en/articles/online-disinformation-unesco-unveils-action-plan-regulate-social-media-platforms

Uncited References

Intelligent agent. (2024). In *Wikipedia.* https://en.wikipedia.org/w/index.php?title=Intelligent_agent&oldid=1231991069

O'Brien, H. L. (2018). A holistic approach to measuring user engagement. In *New directions in third wave human-computer interaction: Volume 2-methodologies* (pp. 81–102). Springer.

Zuboff, S. (2019). *The age of surveillance capitalism: The fight for a human future at the new frontier of power* (1st ed.). PublicAffairs.